"What a difference it would make if Scripture informed our participation in and observation of sports: every play, every game, every season could be a heart-revealing, character-developing experience for the glory of God. In this book, Stephen Altrogge shows us how to bring Scripture into the game—and apply it to our hearts. Full of personal anecdotes and recollections of some of the greatest moments in recent sports history, *Game Day* is a biblical and insightful playbook for anyone who loves to play or watch sports."

—C. J. MAHANEY, Sovereign Grace Ministries

"A new, eye-opening look into sports and the gift from God that sports really are. It has helped adjust my perspective to see how God uses sports to reveal the hidden sin in my heart."

—STEVE BOSDOSH, *Golf Magazine* Top 100 Teacher;
PGA golf instructor; contributor to *Golf Magazine* and
Sports Illustrated

"As I am a father of three boys, pastor and minister to professional athletes, Altrogge's book provided for me sound biblical principles for enjoying the 'game day' as well as seeing sports as a tool for sanctification. I wish Stephen's book were around when Jesus saved my life while playing college football. In a neglected area of discourse *Game Day and the Glory of God* brings a gospel-centered voice to one of America's biggest idols. Humorous stories coupled with serious self-reflection, this work is a valuable resource to have as well as a practical guide to many aspects of ministry."

—GARY SHAVEY, pastor at Mars Hill Church and
chaplain for the Seattle Mariners

"What a wonderful and refreshing take on sports that brings God to the position where he should be: Head Coach, Manager, Commissioner! Stephen makes clear God is in every part of our sporting lives. We may think the score of the game is important, but God is only concerned about the score of the game in victory over the enemy (that does not mean the Cowboys). This book is a blessing for anyone who has or needs perspective. Stephen himself is blessed, though the Lord has placed on his heart the Pittsburgh Pirates."

—DAVID STEIN, talk radio host, *A Celebration of Life Through Sports*

"I could relate to a lot of what Stephen wrote on these pages—sports are often just a shrine to Self, and that manifests itself in an all-encompassing desire to be The Best. That said, there is still much to enjoy and value in sports, and this book will help parents, coaches, and young athletes form a biblical perspective on the games they play."

—TED KLUCK, author, ESPN.com contributor

"We're in desperate need of regaining control of our hearts, minds, and bodies when it comes to competitive sports. I love sports—especially basketball. But as a player and now a fan, I've often participated in ways just shy of insanity. Stephen Altrogge helps a fan like me, players just beginning or in their prime, coaches, and parents approach the enjoyment of sports in their right mind— which is to say with the glory and enjoyment of God as their highest goal. I needed this book as a teenager and now as a parent of young athletes. I plan to share this with the many parents in my church as well. Thanks, Stephen, for pointing us to the Source of our giftedness and joy in sports, God himself."

—THABITI ANYABWILE, Senior Pastor, First Baptist Church,
Grand Cayman Islands

"A must-read for all kinds of athletes, from high school on up through the professional ranks. Drawing from the personal experience of his lifelong love affair with sports, as well as his practical knowledge of Scripture, Stephen Altrogge shows how the sins and temptation that often come with competition can be redeemed for the glory of God."

—PHILIP GRAHAM RYKEN, Senior Minister,
Tenth Presbyterian Church, Philadelphia

"At a time when sport supplants religion and athletes are reverenced as heroes, it does us good to consider if and how we can use sports to bring honor to God. In *Game Day and the Glory of God*, Stephen Altrogge does just that, exploring both the benefits and challenges that await those of us who enjoy the action and drama of sports. Stephen relies on the Bible's timeless wisdom to guide us to a deeper appreciation of God and a deeper abiding in the truths of the gospel on game day and every day."

—TIM CHALLIES, blogger; editor at www.discerningreader.com

"Many Christians have felt vaguely embarrassed by their love of sports, thinking that it is somehow unspiritual. Stephen Altrogge clears away the confusion by showing how sports are gifts from God to be enjoyed. He even shows us how to play the game for God's glory and our own spiritual growth. The next time the umpire cries out, 'Play ball!' we can take the field with excitement, knowing that competition can be good for the soul and can actually bring us closer to God."

—DR. RAY PRITCHARD, President, Keep Believing Ministries;
author, *Credo: Believing in Something to Die For*,
An Anchor for the Soul, and *Fire and Rain:
The Wild-Hearted Faith of Elijah*

GAME DAY

FOR THE GLORY OF

GOD

A Guide for Athletes, Fans, & Wannabes

STEPHEN ALTROGGE

CROSSWAY BOOKS
WHEATON, ILLINOIS

To my wife,
Jen,
the love of my life

2019

Sam,
Continue to
follow your heart,
play + run for Him —
demonstrating what
it is to be a
true Christian Athlete.

Jan Jared
Libby +
CM
Coaches

CONTENTS

FOREWORD

This is the book I needed way back when. I grew up passionate about sports. I played baseball, basketball, and football, and I swam competitively. And when I wasn't playing sports, I was watching sports. Sadly, I think it was all a waste.

Yep, all of it. I wasted my sports because I didn't play for the glory of God. I played for the glory of C. J. Like I said, I wish I'd had this book years ago. (Being a Christian would have helped as well!)

I wasted years of playing sports. But it can be different for you. And it will be, if you will read and apply the contents of this unique book. My friend Stephen Altrogge has given us a book we desperately need, on a topic rarely addressed. He applies the gospel not just to our behavior, but to our hearts. He is theologically informed, reminding us that sports are gifts from God and potential means to grow in godliness. Whether it's a real sport like basketball, soccer, or golf or a bogus sport like Frisbee golf, Stephen wants us to glorify God when we play. (And if you think Frisbee golf is actually a sport, we need to talk.)

So whether you are an athlete (like me), a wannabe (like my friends), a parent, a coach, or simply a fan, *Game Day for the Glory of God* will provide you with a biblical perspective on sports. In the light of the gospel, you will see game day—and yes, even practice—as a moment of eternal significance, whether you win or lose.

C. J. Mahaney
Sovereign Grace Ministries

ACKNOWLEDGMENTS

This book is the result of the unmerited kindness of God upon a wicked sinner. Apart from God drawing me to himself, opening my eyes to the gospel, and putting his Spirit within me, this book would never have been written. And if God had not given me the gift of communication, this book would be nothing more than an idea in my head. So I want to begin by transferring all glory to God for any good that is accomplished by this book.

God was also kind to give me many friends that helped me during and after the writing process. Thanks to my dad for being the editor of my first draft and pushing me to be more creative. Thanks to Justin Taylor for making this book happen. Apart from your help, my friend, this book simply wouldn't exist. Thanks to Ted Griffin for being a patient, joyful, flexible editor.

I'm deeply grateful to C. J. Mahaney, Phil Ryken, Tim Challies, Steve Bosdosh, David Stein, and Ted Kluck for making time to read and endorse the manuscript. Thank you for taking time out of your busy schedules to read a book written by an unknown author.

Finally, I must thank my wife Jen. You have graciously freed me to do all that's necessary in writing a book. You and I rejoiced together when I found out that the book was going to be published. You joyfully worked with me on the tedious process of editing the manuscript. Without your loving support I don't think I would have been able to write this book. I love you with all my heart, and this book is dedicated to you.

PREFACE

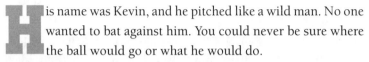

His name was Kevin, and he pitched like a wild man. No one wanted to bat against him. You could never be sure where the ball would go or what he would do.

Yet there I stood in the batter's box, with sweaty palms and cotton mouth, with Kevin standing a mere sixty feet away atop the pitcher's mound. He glared at me with a maniacal, almost homicidal look in his eye, then took the sign from the catcher. I knew what was coming: fastball. That's all Kevin ever threw. The thing that made him tricky to hit was that you were never sure if his blazing fastball was going to pop into the catcher's mitt or slam into your rib cage. He terrified me.

Kevin went into his windup, and my muscles tensed. I was ready for anything. Or so I thought. From the moment the ball left Kevin's hand I could tell that it wasn't going to be a strike. It wasn't even going to be close to a strike. The ball was on a collision course with my head.

As the ball rocketed toward me, my survival instincts kicked in. I turned my body away from the ball, hoping it would deflect off my back rather than my head. No luck. The ball slammed into the back of my head, stunning me. Instantly I crumpled to the ground. It was a brutal collision.

My athletic career has been filled with collisions. Heads crashing together on the basketball court, bodies colliding on the football field, balls knocking me senseless on the baseball diamond. This book is the result of a different type of collision. It's the result of colliding passions. When I was six years old I decided to accept Jesus as my personal Savior. At that moment a passion for God began to blossom in my heart. When I was nine years old I decided to play Little League baseball. It was then that my passion for sports was born.

Up until the age of twelve, the two passions were separate and disconnected. I played baseball, and I went to church. But during my final year of Little League a change began to occur. Until that point I had never played well. When playing baseball it's important to be able to actually hit the ball. This was something I had never quite figured out. I was terrible. I can't count the number of times I walked dejectedly back to the dugout with the words "strike three!" ringing in my ears. The coaches didn't have much faith in me, and I regularly sat the bench. It was very discouraging. Then the miraculous happened. My dad and I began to pray before each game that God would come to my rescue. We prayed that God would infuse my trembling, little arms with power to hit the ball. We prayed that my fielding would improve and that I would find favor in the coaches' eyes. We prayed for supernatural intervention.

God came crashing into my little world of Little League baseball. It was as if something inside me exploded. I started hitting the ball. No, I started *pounding* the ball. Up to that point I had struggled just to make contact. Now I was smashing line drives to the fence. It was like I was on supernatural steroids. That was the turning point in my athletic career. From that point on I was a different athlete. For the first time I began to realize that God might actually care about sports, that the God who created the galaxies and flung the stars into space and sustained the entire universe might care how I, a scrawny twelve-year-old, played baseball. This was a profound revelation.

As I grew older, my passion for God and my passion for sports both increased dramatically. By the age of sixteen I was diligently reading my Bible and diligently playing pickup basketball. But as my passion for both the Lord and sports increased, something else began to happen, something rather disturbing. I started to feel guilty while on the playing field. After a game of pickup basketball I would become painfully aware of ways I had sinned in pride during the game. On other occasions I would feel a black tide of anger rising in my heart if my teammates were playing poorly. Or I would become angry toward an opponent if I felt that he had fouled me unnecessarily hard. I distinctly remember furiously hurling a basketball at one of my friends when he wouldn't stop hacking me during a game. The ball hit him like a punch in the nose, sending him reeling. Fortunately he wasn't hurt. The more I played sports, the more I felt the suffocating weight of my pride and anger. Through all this I came to realize that sports can be played in two ways—for the glory of God or for the glory of self.

My prayer is that God would use this book to help our lives bring maximum glory and honor to him. There are two specific aims for this book. First, my desire is that God would use it to help us enjoy sports as a gift from him. When I say *enjoy*, I don't mean simply playing sports. I mean playing and watching and discussing and thinking about sports. We tend to think of watching a football game as nothing more than a lazy Sunday activity, but God wants us to see it as much more. A game of pickup basketball can be more than a bunch of sweaty, out-of-shape guys missing layups and shooting air balls (at least that's what my games look like). It can be a means of bringing honor, pleasure, and glory to God. Watching *Monday Night Football* can become much more than a night sprawled on the sofa. It can be an act of worship! But for this to happen we must have eyes to see past the gift to the glorious Giver. I pray that by the end of this book we will clearly see the connection between the gift of sports and the glory of God.

Second, my prayer is that we would see sports as a means of growing in godliness. A football game is more than just twenty-two men engaging in sweaty combat on a grass battlefield. A football game is a furnace in which character is formed. The collisions on the field result in more than bruised muscles and busted fingers. They shape our character, in good ways and bad. Out of these collisions come pride, humility, arrogance, courage, perseverance, fear, and a host of other character attributes.

As Christians we are commanded to be like Jesus Christ in every facet of our lives, including the way we play sports. We are to pursue godliness. Godliness doesn't come, however, by just getting out there and playing. You won't pick up a baseball bat, feel a tingling sensation in your fingers, and then suddenly be possessed with a passion for holiness. No, godliness requires intentional and diligent pursuit. Sports provide a context for that to occur. Hebrews 12:14 tells us to "Strive for peace with everyone, and for the holiness without which no one will see the Lord." We are called to strive and strain for holiness with every fiber of our being, remembering that one day we will stand before the Lord himself. May this book be a means of experiencing God's grace in our pursuit of holiness.

I pray that as you read this book you will begin to see sports differently. I pray that you will see sports as more than just a game but as an opportunity. An opportunity to enjoy a wonderful gift from God and an opportunity to grow in godliness. May all we do be for his glory. Amen.

CHAPTER ONE

A LIFE FOR THE GLORY OF GOD

Some moments are frozen in history and burned upon our mind's eye. Moments of ecstatic victory and of heartbreaking defeat. We can see them as clearly as if they happened yesterday. With incredible clarity we can see Michael Jordan using a crossover dribble to free himself from coverage, then draining the game-winning jump shot against the Utah Jazz in game six of the 1998 NBA Finals. We remember Joe Carter thrusting both hands skyward and joyfully leaping into the air after hitting a home run to win the World Series in 1993. Or who can forget the precision-perfect touchdown pass thrown by Pittsburgh Steelers wide receiver Antwaan Randle El to a wide-open Hines Ward in the 2006 Super Bowl?

Of course, not all is glory in the world of sports. We remember the heartbreaks just as well. Tennessee Titans fans shudder when they hear the name Mike Jones. Jones crushed the Titans' hopes of a Super Bowl XXXIV victory when he wrapped his arms around Titans wideout Kevin Dyson as Dyson lunged for what would have been the game-winning touchdown. Pittsburgh Pirate fans curse and spit when they hear the name Francisco Cabrera. It was Cabrera who single-handedly dashed the Pirates' bid for a trip to the 1992 World Series with a clutch pinch-hit single in the bottom of the ninth inning of the National League Championship Series.

We have our own moments of glory and defeat as well. Winning a pickup basketball game with a fadeaway three-pointer. Letting the winning goal slip through our hands in a game of soccer. Running a marathon for the first time. Trying to run a marathon but collapsing in exhaustion before the finish. We cherish the victories and cringe at the defeats.

We live in a world that has fallen madly in love with sports. Every year hundreds of millions of people gather together to play and watch and talk about sports. There are magazines devoted to baseball, football, chess, badminton, poker, Uno, and every other sport imaginable. Stadiums are packed to maximum capacity. Teams that win a championship are given a victory parade and treated like war heroes. Men come together every Saturday to engage in fierce combat on an asphalt battlefield called a basketball court. We seek to improve our holiness and our batting average in church softball leagues. Professional athletes are idolized, and small children can be seen sporting jerseys of their favorite players. Students at the University of West Virginia light couches on fire after thrilling victories. We live in a society that is absolutely crazy about sports, and for many people, sports are their life.

Sports are not merely a modern phenomenon either. For thousands of years athletes have come together to engage in fierce competition. In ancient Rome massive, bloodthirsty crowds would gather to watch gladiators hack each other to pieces with swords. The Olympics were born in ancient Greece, and according to legend the first marathon was also run in ancient Greece. Scripture itself mentions sports in 1 Corinthians 9:24 where Paul says, "Do you not know that in a race all the runners run, but only one receives the prize? So run that you may obtain it."

There is something mystical, almost supernatural about

sports. Something that resonates deep within our hearts. Victory gives us goose bumps and brings us to the verge of tears. We watch in hushed awe as men and women perform athletic feats that seem to defy the laws of physics. Our love for sports often transcends race and politics. We instinctively root for the underdog and are delighted when a weaker team upsets a stronger team. Statistics are our lifeblood. We sometimes have trouble remembering the birthdays of our children but have no problem remembering that Nolan Ryan pitched seven no-hitters. Sports touch us at a deep level, engaging both our hearts and our minds.

DOES GOD REALLY CARE?

As a Christian who absolutely loves sports, I find myself asking several questions. Why did God create sports in the first place? What does God think about sports? Is he interested in our wins and losses and all the organized chaos that happens in between? What are God's priorities in sports? Does the Maker of all things care whether I make my free throws? Does high-sticking bother the High and Exalted One? Is there any connection between Jesus and a jump shot? The answers to these questions are crucial for any Christian who enjoys watching or playing sports.

But before we can determine God's priorities for us in sports we must determine his priorities for us in life. We must first answer the age-old question, why are we here? The answer to this question provides a foundation for answering all other questions. Those who know and embrace God's purpose for their lives will also know and embrace God's purpose for sports. Similarly, those who reject God's purposes for life will also reject God's purposes for sports. Therefore it is absolutely critical that we know why God made us! Those who miss the boat here will find themselves in the dark on every other question of eternal importance.

OUR PURPOSE IN LIFE

Fortunately, God has made things very clear. He hasn't left us to wander hopelessly in the dark. In the Bible we find God's purpose for all men and women clearly spelled out. Isaiah 43:6–7 says, "I will say to the north, Give up, and to the south, Do not withhold; bring my sons from afar and my daughters from the end of the earth, everyone who is called by my name, *whom I created for my glory*, whom I formed and made" (emphasis added).

There it is, the answer to the most important question in all of life! God made you and me for his glory. Our existence isn't the result of a cosmic accident. We are not the by-products of a massive explosion that occurred six billion years ago. No, we were created by God for his glory. To bring something glory means to make it look great. When an Olympic weight lifter wins a gold medal for his country, he brings it glory. He makes his country look really good. After eating a delicious meal we feel compelled to speak. We heap praises on the chef for the tenderness of the steak or the succulence of the apple pie. That brings glory to the chef. It shows just how good the chef really is. God is the most beautiful, amazing, wonderful, glorious being who ever existed, and he has made us to bring honor and worship to him. To do anything else is wicked. First Corinthians 10:31 puts it this way: "So, whether you eat or drink, or whatever you do, do all to the glory of God."

Pretty clear, isn't it? We were created for one all-encompassing purpose: to bring glory to God in all that we do. In his book *Don't Waste Your Life* John Piper puts it this way: "God created me—and you—to live with a single, all-embracing, all-transforming passion—namely, a passion to glorify God by enjoying and displaying his supreme excellence in all the spheres of life."[1] The goal of our lives is worship. Scripture calls us to live in such a way that everything we do and say is worship to God! Worship is not simply the songs we sing on Sunday morning. Worship extends to every facet of our lives. Eating a steak or slurping a milkshake or, as Scripture says, "whatever" we do can be a form of worship. That most certainly includes playing, watching, and talking about sports.

Consider this for a moment. Scripture tells us that everything we do is to be done to the glory of God. Every jump shot and every slap shot. Every single and every strikeout. Every victory and every defeat. Whether we ride the bench or start every game of the season, all of it is to be done to the glory of God.

THE PROBLEM

There is a problem, however. A huge problem. That problem is called sin, and it affects every single one of us. Sin is any failure to conform to the moral standards of God. It's breaking God's perfect and holy commandments. It's rebellion against God. Sin is cosmic treason against the King of the Universe. We were made to live for the glory of God and the honor of his name. We were made to bring him pleasure. Yet each one of us has rejected that purpose and has chosen to live our own way, according to our own desires. Romans 3:23 tells us that "all have sinned and fall short of the glory of God." All of us have failed to glorify God in the way that he deserves. He is an infinitely glorious God, worthy of our highest praise and passionate allegiance. We have given him neither. Instead we spat in God's face and spent our passions on sinful, ungodly pleasures. Because God is holy and just, he can't allow such heinous rebellion to go unpunished. He has decreed that the punishment for sin is eternal spiritual death. Those who reject God will spend a blistering eternity in hell, under the wrath of God, receiving the just punishment for their crimes.

Scripture tells us that in addition to being under the wrath of God, we are also slaves to the power of sin. Ephesians 2:1 describes us as being "dead in . . . trespasses and sins," and Titus 3:3 says of us, "For we ourselves were once foolish, disobedient, led astray, slaves to various passions and pleasures, passing our days in malice and envy, hated by others and hating one another." We don't live in a way that glorifies God, nor do we desire to do so. Those who are slaves of sin can't glorify God. They don't even want to glorify God.

BROKEN CISTERNS

It gets worse. Scripture tells us that not only have we committed cosmic treason, but we have also forsaken the fountain of living water. In Jeremiah 2:12–13 we read, "Be appalled, O heavens, at this; be shocked, be utterly desolate, declares the LORD, for my people have committed two evils: they have forsaken me, the fountain of living waters, and hewed out cisterns for themselves, broken cisterns that can hold no water." Sin is forsaking God, the beautiful fountain of living waters, for putrid, muddy, briny water. It's like choosing to eat maggot-infested bread instead of filet mignon. It's as if someone offered us the crown jewels of England and instead we chose a twenty-five-cent trinket from a vending machine. It's irrational. It's foolish. It shocks and appalls the heavens. Sin is utterly wicked. By choosing sin over God we are saying that it's better and more satisfying than God. This is the ultimate lie. God is the sum of all excellent things. He alone can truly satisfy our hungry souls. To say that he's anything less is a grievous insult and the height of wickedness. He must punish such ungodliness. This is a massive problem.

THE SOLUTION

But there is a solution to our problem, and his name is Jesus Christ. God the Father sent his Son Jesus to do what we could never do.

He sent Jesus to live a life of perfect obedience to the law of God. Every thought he ever had, every word he ever spoke, every deed he ever performed brought honor and glory to God. He was perfect in every sense of the word. If anyone had the right to stand before God's throne and say, "I deserve to be rewarded for my obedience," it was Jesus. Then he did the unimaginable. Jesus didn't claim the reward that his perfect obedience deserved. Instead he chose to die a bloody and shameful death on a splintery piece of wood. As he was hanging on the cross, something absolutely astonishing took place: Jesus was punished for our sins. Second Corinthians 5:21 tells us, "For our sake he made him to be sin who knew no sin, so that in him we might become the righteousness of God."

God the Father looked on God the Son as if he had committed our sins. Then the Father poured out his furious wrath on Jesus, crushing him for our sins. Every perverted thought we ever had, every prideful boast we ever made, every venomous word we ever spoke was laid upon Jesus. He took it all, receiving the full hatred of God toward those sins. He completely drained the cup of God's wrath.

Now if we come to God in repentance we can be forgiven of every sin we ever committed or will commit. The unbearable weight of our sins will be removed, and God will credit Jesus' perfect life to us. God will look upon us as if we had never sinned and always perfectly obeyed him. It's an exchange of our sins for Christ's righteousness. God strips us of our filthy rags of sin and wraps us in white robes of righteousness. What a blessed exchange this is!

We who receive Christ's righteousness also receive new spiritual life. Like flowers blooming in a barren wasteland, new desires spring up in our once spiritually dead hearts, desires to please God and obey him. This change is described in Ephesians 2:4–5, which says, "But because of his great love for us, God, who is rich in mercy, made us alive with Christ even when we were dead in transgressions—it is by grace you have been saved" (NIV). Our relationship to God also changes. Before salvation we are enemies of God and under his wrath. After salvation, God adopts us as his children and gives us all the privileges of being sons and daughters of God. What incredible mercy he pours out on us!

This is the foundation of living a life that glorifies God. The gospel of Jesus Christ is what makes it possible for us to glorify and please God in all that we do. Those who aren't reconciled to God cannot obey him. Romans 8:8 says, "Those who are in the flesh cannot please God." The gospel brings forgiveness and new life to our souls, and it empowers us to live in a way that glorifies God.

Throughout the remainder of this book we will be trying to answer the question of how we can enjoy sports for the glory of God. As we take a deeper look we will be made keenly aware of how often we fail to bring God glory. It's at this point that we must return again to the sweet news of the gospel and remember that our acceptance with God is based solely on what Jesus Christ has accomplished. Only then will we have the strength and the courage to confront our failures and seek to change. Only then will we be able to truly glorify God in all of life.

CHAPTER TWO

THE SOURCE OF ALL TALENT

He was incredible. Perhaps the greatest to ever play the game. Unstoppable. Unbeatable. Absolutely unbelievable. He would dazzle you with his high-flying dunks and take your breath away with his acrobatic jump shots. He was consistent throughout the game and killer in the clutch. There was something almost magical about watching him play. You always had the sense that something phenomenal was about to happen when he took the ball in his oversized hands. He redefined the game of basketball and was arguably the greatest player ever to step on a basketball court. He simply dominated. His name? Michael Jordan.

In his book *Playing for Keeps: Michael Jordan and the World He Made*, David Halberstam quotes former Celtics player Danny Ainge, who said the following about Jordan:

> The danger was that he was so good you were tempted to stop playing and just watch. It was not just what he did, but the way he did it. We knew when he had gone into the game that he was very good, but none of us knew yet that he was going to be the best player who ever laced sneakers.[1]

Michael Jordan was a man of remarkable talents. To say that he impressed people would be a colossal understatement. He amazed people. Awed them. Shocked them. Seeing him play the game of basketball was a jaw-dropping experience. During every game there would be at least one moment when you found yourself asking, "How did he do that?" Yes, Michael Jordan was an impressive figure.

But was God impressed by Michael's abilities? Did he gather the angels around the celestial television set and say to them, "You'll never believe what Michael does on this play"? Similarly, is God impressed by our athletic abilities? Even though none of us will ever be Michael Jordan, many of us have been blessed with some degree of athletic ability. Is God impressed by the way I hit a tennis ball or throw a curveball? Many times I think I'm pretty hot stuff. Does God feel the same way? To answer this question we must identify the source of all our talents.

THE SOURCE OF OUR TALENTS

The Bible makes it very clear that we were created by God. In Psalm 139:13–14 David says, "For you formed my inward parts; you knitted me together in my mother's womb. I praise you, for I am fearfully and wonderfully made."

We are the craftsmanship of God. He formed and shaped us in the womb. Our height, weight, eye color, and level of coordination were all determined by God before we were born. It is God who sovereignly decides what our talents and abilities will be. To some he gives the ability to slap a hockey puck into a net at approximately the speed of sound, or at least so it seems. To others he gives extraordinary intellectual firepower, enabling them to quickly solve complex physics equations. Michael Jordan's astonishing abilities were given to him by the Maker of all things. He didn't earn them, nor did he do anything to deserve them. They were generous gifts from a generous God.

Similarly, any athleticism that you possess has been given to you by God as a gift. Can you drive a golf ball 250 yards? That ability is from God. Consider for a moment all that is required to hit a golf ball. It's not enough to simply rear back and swing the club. Driving a golf ball any substantial distance requires precise coordination between the hands, arms, eyes, legs, back, feet, and head. The slightest bending of the head or twisting of the hands can make the difference between a 300-yard drive and a thirty-yard dink. Or consider the simple act of shooting a basketball. Have you ever considered all that occurs in the second it takes to shoot the ball? First, the body must be positioned so that it's facing the basketball hoop. Then the brain must make a split-second judgment to determine the distance between the body and the hoop. Based on the distance to the hoop, the brain instantly calculates the approximate trajectory needed to get the ball into the hoop. The brain then determines how much arm strength and hand movement are needed to get the ball moving toward the basket. Things become increasingly complex as more variables, such as a leaping defender, are thrown into the mix. All this takes place in the blink of an eye. A fadeaway jump shot is truly amazing.

Unfortunately, we often view our athletic abilities through the lens of pride. We seek to draw attention to our athletic prowess and to prove our athletic superiority. We want others to see us play well so they will think highly of us and praise us. Our culture only feeds this tendency. Today's athletes are looked upon as heroes. They star in television commercials and are treated like kings. They get paid millions of dollars to slip on basketball shoes with air in the heels or to eat a specific brand of hot dogs. In short, they are worshiped. How foolish this is! Our athletic abilities were given to us by God as gifts for the purpose of glorifying him. We haven't done anything to earn or deserve them. How can we boast about an undeserved gift? It's like bragging about the color of your hair. How can we bring glory to ourselves when all honor and praise belong to God? In our sinful pride we long to be praised. We want people to see our abilities and praise *us* for them rather than God.

As Christians we're called to put sin to death in every area of our lives, including the area of sports. God is far more concerned with our holiness than with our ability to pluck rebounds out of the air. So how do we fight these sinful tendencies that arise within our hearts? How can we use our athletic abilities in a way that brings honor to our Creator?

GOD IS NOT IMPRESSED

First, we must realize that God isn't impressed with our athletic abilities. My temptation is to be easily astounded by my own abilities, meager though they may be. Let me paint a scenario for you. I've just finished playing a game of pickup basketball on a Saturday morning. I played pretty well, making some difficult shots and playing decent defense. In my head a highlight reel of my top ten plays of the day is rolling, and I can almost hear the ESPN *SportsCenter* music playing in the background. I'm feeling good, impressed with myself and confident that those around me were also impressed. My pride is swelling like an overinflated basketball.

But God isn't impressed. The Maker of all things isn't amazed when I rattle in three consecutive jump shots. The ruler of heaven and earth isn't awestruck by my ability to hurl a baseball or hit a golf ball. In fact, when I compare myself to God I find that I am very small and insignificant. When I compare my achievements to God's achievements, I find that I have no reason to be proud. Consider Isaiah 40:12, which says, "Who has measured the waters in the hollow of his hand and marked off the heavens with a span, enclosed the dust of the earth in a measure and weighed the mountains in scales and the hills in a balance?"

God holds all the waters of the earth in the palm of his hand. The vast oceans of the world are nothing more than a drop of water when compared to him. He spans the galaxies with his thumb and little finger. The entire universe is nothing more than a hand width across for him. I can't even palm a basketball; God can palm the universe. Do I really think that God is going to be blown away by my talent? Can I truly believe for even a second that God, who holds the stars in place, would be wowed by my ability to swing a tennis racket? Not a chance. God isn't impressed by me, nor is he impressed by you. Even the greatest athletes in the world are nothing when compared to the One who made the world. God is great, we are not, and he has created us so that we might show him to be exceedingly great. We should desire that people would be amazed at God, not at us. To hunger for the praise of others is to desire what belongs to God alone.

Take a moment to ask yourself, do I play sports in a way that draws undue attention to myself? Do I desire that people would be amazed by my abilities? Am I impressed with myself? If you answered yes to any of these questions (and I answered yes to all three), then pride has taken root in your heart, and you are stealing the praise that belongs to God alone.

THE COMPARISON GAME

A second way to use our talents for the glory of God is to avoid the comparison game. By its very nature sports involves comparisons. Some teams are better than others, and some players are better than others. The Pittsburgh Steelers won the Super Bowl in 2006 (which happened to fulfill one of my lifelong dreams). The Pittsburgh Pirates, on the other hand, could be beaten by a team of prepubescent sixth graders. Some consider Ted Williams to be the greatest hitter to ever play the game of baseball. Others would argue that Ty Cobb should be given that honor. Sports always generates comparisons. They aren't necessarily wrong.

It is wrong, however, to compare yourself to others for the purpose of exalting yourself. In Luke 14:11 we read, "For everyone who exalts himself will be humbled, and he who humbles himself will be exalted." Personally I find this to be a particularly strong temptation. After playing sports I often find myself mentally comparing my performance to the performances of those around me. If I played better than everyone else, I feel happy. If I played poorly, however, I tend to feel discouraged.

It's all rather silly when I sit and think about it. Why does it matter if I played better than those around me? I'm not trying out for the NBA or trying to make an All-Star Game. I don't have any shoe deals or television endorsements riding on my performance, and I certainly don't have any money at stake. So what's the big deal?

The big deal is my sinful, self-glorifying pride. I want to be the best, and I want others to recognize me as the best. The best athletes get glory, praise, and free Gatorade, all of which I desperately want. I want others to think of me as an exceptional athlete, far above average. I want to be the guy who gets picked first in pickup basketball. What it boils down to is that I want to be worshiped. Of course, I would never say this, but my thoughts and actions reveal what's really in my heart. In these instances I'm more concerned with my glory than with God's glory. By comparing myself to others I'm seeking to exalt myself so I will receive praise and recognition. Again, I want the praise that belongs to God alone.

Do you ever find yourself playing the comparison game? Do you compare yourself to others, hoping you are the best? Beware of this sinful arrogance. God is the one who sovereignly determined the talents you would receive. You did nothing to deserve or earn them. They all came as gifts from the generous hand of God. There is no boasting over gifts.

On the other hand, do you ever find yourself discontented with the talents you possess? Are you ever unhappy because you are not a better athlete? Do you wish you could be like someone else? This doesn't please God either. He gave you the exact abilities he wanted you to have, no more and no less. In his glorious wisdom and sovereignty, he created each of us with a unique set of gifts. Discontentment says that we're not happy with the way God made us. We're saying that God made a mistake when he created us. We're saying that he didn't know what was best for us. When we do this we're sinning greatly against him.

Playing the comparison game only leads to pride or discontentment. By the grace of God, let us avoid the temptation to compare ourselves to others.

A THANKFUL HEART

We can also glorify God by giving thanks for the athletic abilities he has given us. How simple this is; yet how often it is overlooked. In Psalm 69:30 David says, "I will praise the name of God with a song; *I will magnify him with thanksgiving*" (emphasis added). As mentioned in the previous chapter, each of us has rebelled against God and deserves an eternity in hell. But praise God, he has not given us what we deserve. Instead of casting us into hell, he punished Jesus in our place. He has forgiven our sins and washed our consciences clean. To top it all off, he pours blessing after blessing upon us!

One of those blessings is the ability to play and watch sports. Consider how much joy comes from playing sports. The thrill of sinking a thirty-foot putt on a twisted green or hitting a game-winning single. The breathless satisfaction that comes from finishing a marathon. The pleasure of throwing a hard-breaking curveball. Consider also the joy that's found in watching sports. The heart-pounding pleasure of seeing a game-winning field goal and the euphoria of watching a buzzer-beating three-pointer. Or the sense of awe at seeing a professional basketball player make a thunderous, rim-rattling dunk. These are all sweet pleasures indeed, given to us by an incredibly lavish and generous God.

Yet how often do we give thanks to God for these pleasures? How often do we thank God for allowing us to play football or baseball? How often do we praise him for the sweet pleasure of skiing through twelve inches of fresh powder? I take particular delight in college basketball, especially during the month of March. I love the suspense surrounding the NCAA Tournament selection process. Will my team make it, or will they have to settle for the NIT Tournament? I love filling out a tournament bracket and trying to determine which team has the perfect mixture of toughness and talent to become a national champion. I delight in the colossal upsets that always occur, such as when little-known George Mason University beat the powerhouse University of Connecticut to advance to the Final Four championship round in 2006. March is a thrilling month.

Unfortunately, I rarely find myself uttering even a word of thanks to God for these pleasures. I have done nothing to deserve them. My sins merit eternal punishment in hell. Instead, God plucked me out of the darkness, made me his son, and heaped blessing after extravagant blessing upon me, including sports. As I loaf on my couch and watch basketball, I'm experiencing the goodness and kindness of God toward me. Because of his love for me he allows me to experience great pleasure and joy as I watch sports. My heart should be overflowing with gratitude to God for his incredible mercy.

How about you? Is watching and playing sports an occasion for gratitude? Do you ever find yourself lifting thanksgiving or praise to God after you have played sports? Have you ever thanked God for the astonishing amounts of joy that you receive through something as simple as sports? God will be honored and glorified if you do! He is magnified and seen as glorious by our thanksgiving. It's very easy to watch and play sports without giving a single thought to the One who created them. Let us fight this sinful tendency by thanking God for the wonderful gift of sports.

THE SOURCE OF OUR JOY

As we conclude this chapter, let us consider the One who created sports. Let us look beyond the gift to the Giver himself. How great our God must be! If we receive such intense pleasure from sports, what must the One who invented all sports be like? If we receive such joy from watching Michael Jordan play basketball, what must the God who gave Michael his incredible talents be like? God created sports to bring joy to millions of people. Yet infinitely more joy is found in God himself. Thankfully, sports are not our ultimate joy. How shallow and short-lived that joy would be. God is our ultimate joy and deepest satisfaction.

CHAPTER THREE

THE JOY OF SPORTS

R unning is a painful thing for me. My chest hurts. My feet ache. The muscles in my legs tighten up. By the end of the run I usually have two main concerns: either my heart is beating with such intensity that I'm concerned it might burst and I will die, or I cannot fill my lungs with enough oxygen to keep me from passing out and/or dying. But there is also something very pleasurable about running. Running brings a sense of freedom, as if I'm throwing off restraints. As I feel the wind blowing against me and see the pavement gliding beneath me, I begin to experience pleasure along with the pain. Eric Liddell would have understood. Eric was a runner, a blazing fast runner, and he knew that it was God who made him fast. For Eric, running wasn't about getting in shape or losing weight. It was all about pleasure. In the classic movie *Chariots of Fire*, Eric makes the following profound statement:

> I believe God made me for a purpose, but he also made me fast. And when I run I feel His pleasure.[1]

When Eric ran, he sensed God's pleasure! Speed was God's gift to Eric, and Eric took immense pleasure in that gift. He viewed his speed as a gift from God to be thoroughly enjoyed. Have you ever experienced that wonderful sense of pleasure of which Eric spoke?

Have you ever had that feeling of glory, of being incredibly alive, that comes from playing sports? When all your muscles are working together and your heart is pounding like a hot rod engine and every sense is sharpened? It's a glorious thing. Sports are clearly gifts from God to us.

But why is it that we feel such joy in sports? What is it that brings us to our feet when we see a basketball player soar through the air for a rim-rocking dunk? What is it that makes us smile when we smash a golf ball down the fairway? Why is there such pleasure in playing touch football in a muddy backyard with our friends? Throughout this chapter we'll consider these questions so that we might enjoy the gift of sports in ways that please and honor God.

THE JOY OF EXCELLENCE

There is something in us that is irresistibly drawn toward excellence. We can't help but gaze in wonder at a masterful piece of artwork. Our hearts are captivated by the glorious strains of music created by a symphony. A thanksgiving turkey roasted to golden-brown perfection receives our emphatic praise. Everywhere you look people and companies are engaged in the passionate pursuit of excellence, and nowhere is this more clearly displayed than in the arena of sports. Every player is in search of the "perfect swing" or the "perfect shot" or even the "perfect season." Day in and day out players push their bodies to the limit in an effort to sharpen their athletic skills. Some coaches have taken the pursuit of excellence to the extreme, cursing and screaming at their players over even the smallest mistakes. As spectators we are also enraptured by excellence. We can't help but be dazzled as we watch an Olympic sprinter run a blazing 100 meters in under ten seconds or see Chicago Bulls guard Ben Gordon knock down nine consecutive three-point shots. There is something awe-inspiring about watching St. Louis Cardinals first baseman Albert Pujols swat mammoth home runs or seeing Tiger Woods absolutely murder a golf ball. Excellence is attractive.

Why are we so drawn to excellence? At first glance this might seem like an odd question. Why would we not be drawn to excellence? It's almost like asking why a man would be attracted to a woman. It's just the way it is. Or is it? I believe that the answer is not as simple as we might think. It goes much deeper and is rooted in the very character of God.

God is the most excellent, glorious being who exists. In Matthew 5:48 Jesus tells us, "Your heavenly Father is perfect." Stop and ponder that word "perfect" for a moment. God is perfection. His love is the sweetest and most tender love that has ever been known. It is perfect love. His power is both awe-inspiring and terrifying. It is perfect power. His wisdom, which infinitely exceeds all the wisdom collected by men through the ages, is perfect wisdom. He is perfect in every facet of his character, and all that he does flows out of his excellence.

All of creation has been kissed by the glory of God and gives us a small glimpse into his character. Even though creation has been marred and distorted by sin, we can still see the glory of God piercing through. When we hear a bird lifting its voice in beautiful song or see a breathtaking sunrise, we are glimpsing the character of God. He created the singing bird and the golden hues of a sunrise. If we get such pleasure from these things, what must the God who created them be like? He must be the most excellent of all! The glories of creation are meant to direct our attention to the glorious Creator. C. S. Lewis put it this way:

> I was standing today in the dark toolshed. The sun was shining outside and through the crack at the top of the door there

came a sunbeam. From where I stood that beam of light, with the specks of dust floating in it, was the most striking thing in the place. Everything else was almost pitch-black. I was seeing the beam, not seeing things by it. Then I moved so that the beam fell on my eyes. Instantly the whole previous picture vanished. I saw no toolshed, and (above all) no beam. Instead I saw, framed in the irregular cranny at the top of the door, green leaves moving on the branches of a tree outside and beyond that, 90 odd million miles away, the sun. Looking along the beam, and looking at the beam are very different experiences.[2]

Lewis understood that we must look through the "beam" of God's good gifts to see their glorious source. We see this again in James 1:17, which reads, "Every good gift and every perfect gift is from above, coming down from the Father of lights with whom there is no variation or shadow due to change." Behind every good gift in creation is a generous and glorious God.

This applies to sports as well. Professional baseball players are incredible. It amazes me to see a person hurl a ball at ninety miles an hour with sniper-like accuracy. I can't throw a baseball that hard. My arm would fall off if I tried. My flimsy arm simply lacks the power. The arm of a Major League pitcher is like a stick of dynamite—absolutely packed with power. Now consider God himself. If God has given such power to frail human beings, how much more powerful must he be? A Major League pitcher is throwing a small, white sphere that weighs a mere five ounces. God threw the planets into orbit. Even the best pitchers lack the ability to control their pitches at times. God holds the universe together and keeps the planets in orbit. Humans have some power. God is infinitely powerful.

I'm even more amazed by professional golfers. My body refuses to play golf. When I pick up a golf club, I lose all control of my hands and arms. I look like I'm having a mild seizure when I swing the club. When I hit the ball, there's no guarantee that it will go straight, or even forward. Watching Tiger Woods play golf is a different story. He has mastered his body, and it does his bidding. His swing is ferocious, his putts delicate. He makes his opponents look like putt-putt golfers. The excellence of Tiger, however, is but the faintest whisper of God's excellence. Tiger Woods makes mistakes. He slices balls into the trees and misses easy putts. He occasionally chokes in the clutch. But God never makes mistakes, and he does all things with excellence! I experience joy in watching Tiger Woods because I'm catching a very faint glimpse of the glory and excellence of God.

This should greatly affect the way we play and watch sports. When we excel at sports, we are in a very small way reflecting the excellence of God's character. This is part of the reason why we experience so much joy in playing sports. Doing things excellently is a reflection of God, who does all things with excellence. The same is true of watching sports. When we see an athlete perform exceptionally well, we're seeing a small portion of God's character.

For example, in the 1982 NFC Championship game, Joe Montana and Dwight Clark connected for what has since become known simply as "The Catch." With less than a minute remaining in the game and the Forty-Niners trailing 27-21, Montana lined up on the Cowboys' six-yard line. As soon as the ball was snapped, Montana was under pressure. The Forty-Niners' front line collapsed, and Montana found himself face to face with three Cowboy defenders. He rolled to his right, under hot pursuit from the defense, desperately looking for an open receiver. At the last possible second Montana floated a pass to the back right corner of the end zone in the general direction of Forty-Niners receiver Dwight Clark. Clark launched himself into the air and managed to snag the pass with his outstretched fingertips, winning the NFC championship for the Forty-Niners and securing for himself a place in football lore.[3] Clark's catch was a thing of beauty and was a reflection of the excellence of God.

The application of this truth is simple. When you play sports well, turn your heart to God and praise him for his excellence. Acknowledge that he's the only one who does all things well. Acknowledge that your ability to do things with excellence is nothing compared to his ability to do things with excellence. Respond by thanking him for the abilities that he's given to you and remembering that all talent comes from him. Similarly, when you're watching sports and see an athlete make a play that brings your hands up and your jaw down, let that direct your thoughts to God. Take a moment to praise him for the gifts that he's given to men, and praise him for his superior excellence. For those of you who play organized sports, let this motivate you to practice hard. We can glorify God through the pursuit of excellence, and excellence only comes through hard work. God isn't glorified by halfhearted, mediocre efforts. So work hard in practice, not for your own honor and praise, but for the glory of God.

THE JOY OF VICTORY

Why is it that we love victory? Why is it that within minutes of sitting down to watch a game, I find myself instinctively rooting for one team over another, even if I have no connection to either team? What is it that drives men and women to sacrifice their time, energy, friends, family, social life, and even spiritual life in the pursuit of victory? Why do we take our passion to win into the smallest and most insignificant portions of our lives? We play Monopoly as if it were the Super Bowl and play Life as if it really were life. We love to win.

Unfortunately, our passion for victory is not pure in any sense. We are arrogant and proud and often desire victory solely for the praise it will bring us. Losers have never been admired throughout history, and we certainly don't want to be lumped in with those chumps. But does this mean that it's wrong to desire victory at all? Should we desire to lose? I don't believe so. In victory we see a snapshot of the nature and character of God.

We live in a world that's opposed to God. Like a great plague, sin has ravaged all of creation. Scripture tells us that those who don't know Christ are enemies of God and hostile toward him. Satan prowls about like a rabid lion, seeking to oppose all that God does and to destroy the faith of Christians. Suffering permeates all of life, and tragedies are a regular occurrence. It would seem that evil is winning all the battles.

But Scripture paints a very different picture for us. It acknowledges that evil has filled the earth, but it doesn't stop there. It tells us about a God who is always the victor and conqueror. His plans can't be thwarted, and he always triumphs over his enemies. In Psalm 110:1 we read, "The LORD says to my Lord: 'Sit at my right hand, until I make your enemies your footstool.'" In 2 Corinthians 2:14 Paul says, "But thanks be to God, who in Christ always leads us in triumphal procession, and through us spreads the fragrance of the knowledge of him everywhere."

We serve a God who always conquers his enemies! None can stand against him or stop his glorious purposes. He's an unbeatable and unstoppable warrior. His victory is inevitable. Evil will not ultimately triumph in this world. At the cross, Christ secured the final victory for all of God's people and broke the power of Satan. A day is soon coming when Christ will return, and evil will be vanquished once and for all. Satan will be flung into the Lake of Fire, and the wicked will receive just punishment for the evils they've committed. The final victory of God is secure. He has already won and is now in the process of finishing off his enemies.

We live in a world that's rife with evil, and our hearts are longing for good to triumph. We want assurance that evil won't have the final victory and that good will emerge from all the pain. In God we find that victory.

Victory in sports is a faint reflection of our victorious God. He's created us to love victory. No one enjoys losing. Part of the reason we have such a passion for victory is that it allows us to catch a faint glimpse of God's glory. Granted, our motives for wanting victory are often smeared with pride and arrogance. But victory in and of itself can be something very good. God is the great warrior king, the great victor and conqueror. When we witness victory, we are witnessing a small piece of the character of God.

We also love victory because it proves that diligence is rewarded. Throughout Scripture we are told that God is pleased by those who do their work faithfully. Proverbs 13:4 says, "The soul of the sluggard craves and gets nothing, while the soul of the diligent is richly supplied." Impressive victories rarely come without hours of grueling work and preparation. The best teams in sports are those that sweat blood on the practice field. They run the same drill over and over until they can do it in their sleep. They spend hours in darkened rooms analyzing film of the opposing team, so that by the time game day rolls around they're ready for anything. It's good and God-honoring to see a team's hard work pay off, and nothing is more unsatisfying than seeing a team get a win they didn't deserve. In a sense we want to see good triumph over evil in this situation as well. We certainly want to see hard work triumph over laziness. We want to see diligence and perseverance have the final victory.

So by all means, pursue victory! Pursue the joy that God gives to the victorious. Not for your own glory or honor, but because in victory you will see a glimpse of God himself. When you find yourself on a winning team, direct your heart and mind to God, and praise him that he is always victorious. Thank him for the joy that comes with victory. Praise him for the victories that he's achieved in your life. Praise him that he always leads you in his triumph. Acknowledge that he's the only one who never loses and is always victorious. Pursue victory for the glory of God.

THE JOY OF SELF-FORGETFULNESS

Not only do we receive joy as we pursue excellence and victory, but sports also bring us joy by giving us temporary self-forgetfulness. This idea may sound odd to some, so let me take a moment to explain.

Have you ever had a moment when you were so engrossed with something that you completely forgot about yourself? Something that grabbed your attention so forcefully that you forgot about your wants and worries and desires? This happened to me several years ago during a trip my brother and I took to Yellowstone National Park. Several times while hiking through the park we came upon scenes so beautiful that they stopped us in our tracks and caused us to stare in wonder. Snowcapped mountains, crystal streams, and deep, meandering valleys riveted our attention with their astonishing beauty and caused our hearts to be filled with praise for the God who made them. The effect of all this was that I often simply forgot about myself and the things that concerned me. My eyes and thoughts were fixed on the glories that surrounded me and the God who created them all.

In Psalm 8:3–4 David tells of a similar experience he had when gazing up into the night sky. He says, "When I look at your heavens, the work of your fingers, the moon and the stars, which you have set in place, what is man that you are mindful of him, and the son of man that you care for him?" David was lost in wonder as he gazed up at the starry sky and contemplated the infinite glory of God.

It's good for us to forget about our needs and desires from time to time. By nature we're very selfish and are inclined to think only of ourselves. Our society tells us that life is all about us. It encourages our selfishness. Sports, however, like nature, provide us an opportunity to fix our attention on something other than ourselves. They demand our fullest attention for a short span of time, and as we focus on the game itself we tend to temporarily forget about ourselves. Granted, there are many times when sin invades our self-forgetfulness and once again turns our focus inward, like when we feel that we're not getting the ball enough in a game of basketball. But in general, sports allow us to be self-forgetful, and that's a wonderful gift from God. There is something very healthy, mentally and emotionally, about self-forgetfulness. In his book *The Hidden Smile of God* John Piper says: "Periodic self-examination is needed and wise and biblical. But for the most part, mental health is the use of the mind to focus on worthy reality outside ourselves."[4]

Isn't God kind to give us the gifts of sports? They allow us to focus our minds on a reality that's completely outside ourselves. When I play pickup basketball, I'm temporarily transported out of the swirling mass of subjective thoughts and emotions that would normally occupy my mind and into a rock-solid world of layups, rebounds, and crossover dribbles. This is a very good thing indeed. Self-centeredness only leads to unhappiness and misery. Sports are gifts from God that allow us to temporarily forget about self.

THE JOY OF CHARACTER

Finally, sports provide us a wonderful means of growing in character. Sports aren't just about swatting a ball with a racket or slapping a puck into a net. Playing sports allows us to develop character traits that will help us throughout our entire lives. Take leadership, for example. Have you ever considered how much leadership is required when playing sports? Like a general commanding an army, a quarterback is the leader of his team, and players look to him for direction. Veterans lead rookies. Strong players lead weak players. Teams that must depend on young and inexperienced players often suffer due to a lack of leadership. If you play sports you are bound to end up in a position of leadership at some point. Learning to lead on the field has tremendous ramifications for what takes place off the field. Businesses need leaders. Churches need godly leaders. God calls men to be leaders in their households. In his kindness, God allows men and boys to learn to lead by playing sports.

At this point let me appeal to fathers. Fathers, help your sons be leaders on the playing field. A leader encourages his teammates and seeks to fire their passion for excellence. He sets an example of hard work for his teammates and humbly encourages others to follow his example. A leader respects his coaches and listens attentively to their correction. Fathers, help your sons be this kind of leader.

Sports also teach the value of perseverance. We live in an emotionally fragile, escapist culture that likes to curl up in the fetal position when things get tough. The Christian attitude, however, should be distinctly different. Hebrews 12:1 tells us, "Therefore, since we are surrounded by so great a cloud of witnesses, let us also lay aside every weight, and sin which clings so closely, and *let us run with endurance* the race that is set before us" (emphasis added).

Living a life for the glory of God requires endurance. It's not easy to be a Christian. Killing sin is difficult. Pressing on through trials is painful. Contrary to what some pastors are teaching today, Christians aren't immune from pain and trials. In 1 Peter 4:12 we read, "Beloved, do not be surprised at the fiery trial when it comes upon you to test you, as though something strange were happening to you." Christians will endure suffering and trials. God calls us to endure such difficulties by his Spirit, so that he might be glorified.

Playing sports helps us learn the value of endurance. Football players must endure excruciating heat and the perils of dehydration during summer football camps. Distance runners must learn to ignore the shooting pains that often seize them in the middle of a race. Heroes emerge by playing through pain. In the 1988 World Series Kirk Gibson became a legend by hitting a game-winning home run in the first game of the series. He wasn't in good health that night. A ripped hamstring and a torn knee were causing him such agony that he didn't even bother to suit up for the game. But by the bottom of the ninth inning Gibson's Dodgers were desperate. Down 4-3, they had one man on and two outs. The Oakland Athletics had their sidearm ace, Dennis Eckersley, on the mound. Dodgers manager Tommy Lasorda asked hitting coach Ben Hines to check on Gibson and see if he might be able to pinch-hit. After checking on Gibson, Hines came back to Lasorda and told him, "He thinks he's got one good swing in him." Lasorda decided to bring him in. Geoffrey Ward and Ken Burns tell us what happened next:

> Gibson hobbled to the plate and waited. He knew he'd have just one chance. Eckersley fired five pitches past him. Gibson's bat never left his shoulder. The count was three and two. Then, Eckersley tried a slider. Gibson hurled himself into the pitch and knocked it into the tenth row of the bleachers. . . . It was

Gibson's only at-bat in the series, but the inspired Dodgers went on to beat the unnerved A's in five games.[5]

God has given us sports to help us learn endurance. Learning to persevere through the pain of sports teaches us how to persevere through the pain of life. This doesn't mean, however, that God-glorifying endurance comes from sheer willpower. Many non-Christians persevere through pain and difficulty without ever glorifying God. God-glorifying endurance is the fruit of a heart that's dependent on God. We glorify God when we persevere through difficulty by his strength rather than our own. What does this look like practically? It looks like praying for strength to continue practicing when our body wants to quit. It looks like praying for endurance to continue running hard in the fourth quarter even when our lungs are on fire. It looks like finding strength from God to practice hard even though you may not get into a single game the entire season. Endurance that glorifies God is dependent on God.

God has given us the gift of sports so that we might learn endurance and perseverance. Let's resolve to find our strength in him on game day. When we find that our strength has vanished and five minutes still remain on the clock, let's turn to God for strength. Parents, you can help your children in this area. When they're tempted to give up after striking out for the fifth time in a row, help them persevere. Direct their attention to the only One who can truly strengthen them. Then take them out to the batting cages and make them hit a hundred balls.

A FITTING RESPONSE

Millions of people around the world take immense pleasure in playing and watching sports. But how many of those people ever thank the One who created sports? How often do I lift my voice in thanksgiving after playing a game of softball or a round of golf? Do I ever thank God for the incredible amount of pleasure that I receive from sports? Unfortunately, I often enjoy the gift of sports without ever thanking the creator of sports. This should not be.

Let us resolve from this point forward that we will not enjoy the gift of sports without giving thanks and honor to the Giver himself. Let us recognize that sports are indeed gifts from a generous God to undeserving sinners, and let our enjoyment of sports be marked by thankful hearts. In this way we will enjoy sports for the glory of God.

CHAPTER FOUR

GAME DAY PRIORITIES

O n August 7, 2007 Barry Bonds did his home run trot for the 756th time in his career. After many seasons of putting up staggering home run totals, Bonds finally passed Hank Aaron as the all-time home run leader in Major League baseball, and wrote his name into the record books. In recent years allegations have arisen that Barry, along with many other Major League baseball players, took performance-enhancing steroids. Now fans no longer cheer when Bonds steps into the batter's box. They call him a cheater. They throw syringes at him. Many believe that his name should go into the record books accompanied by an asterisk, indicating that he was only able to set the home run record by using steroids. In their book *Game of Shadows*, Mark Fainaru-Wada and Lance Williams make the following comment about Barry Bonds:

> For as long as he had played baseball, Bonds had regarded himself as better than every other player he encountered, and almost always he was right. But as the 1998 season ended, Bonds's elite status had slipped a notch. The game and its fans were less interested in the complete player who could hit for average and power and who had great speed and an excellent glove. The emphasis was shifting to pure slugging . . . as [Mark] McGwire was celebrated as the best slugger of the modern era and perhaps the greatest who

had ever lived, Bonds became more jealous than people who knew him well had ever seen.[1]

I can relate to Barry Bonds. In my sinful pride, I also want to be great in the world's eyes. I want to be a successful athlete and don't like being second to anyone. I want people to think of me as a great athlete and a consistent winner. I absolutely hate losing. It makes me look bad. And I'm not alone either. For many individuals, success is the number one priority. Our culture defines athletic success in two ways: victory and personal statistics. These are the number one and number two priorities for most athletes.

As Christians, however, we should have a different set of priorities. As was mentioned in the first chapter of this book, our greatest passion should be honoring and glorifying God. All other passions and priorities should flow out of this one, all-consuming passion. Our desire to win or to play well must be directed by our passion to glorify God. Therefore, it's critical that we determine what matters to God when we're playing sports. We must answer the question, what does God care about when I'm on the playing field? Throughout the remainder of this chapter we will seek to answer this question.

THE PRIORITY OF HUMILITY

When humility shows up on the playing field, it's tough to ignore. In fact, humility has become somewhat of a rarity in today's world of professional sports. The National Football League is a prime example of this. In recent years end-zone celebrations following a touchdown have become increasingly extravagant and flashy. Following one touchdown catch, the now infamous wide receiver Terrell Owens whipped a marker out of his sock, autographed the football, and then handed it to a fan sitting in the stands. Not to be outdone, New Orleans Saints wide receiver Joe Horn pulled out a cell phone that he had hidden by one of the field goalposts and made a call to his mother, informing her that he had just caught a touchdown pass. Things have gotten so bad in recent seasons that the NFL has begun fining players for excessive celebration in the end zone. It seems safe to say that in at least some of these cases the players lack humility.

For Christians this shouldn't be the case. Scripture makes it very clear that God is drawn to the humble and opposes the proud. In Isaiah 66:1–2 we read:

> Thus says the LORD: "Heaven is my throne, and the earth is my footstool; what is the house that you would build for me, and what is the place of my rest? All these things my hand has made, and so all these things came to be, declares the LORD. But this is the one to whom I will look: he who is humble and contrite in spirit and trembles at my word."

God isn't drawn to the chest-thumping, loud-mouthing, self-proclaiming athlete who boasts about himself. He's not drawn to the person with the smoothest jump shot or sweetest golf swing. He's not impressed with the seventy-three home runs that Barry Bonds hit in a single season or the 4,256 hits amassed by Pete Rose throughout his career. What impresses God is humility. God is drawn toward those who humbly acknowledge that he is great and they are not. God isn't drawn to our talent or intelligence. It's the humble and contrite person who attracts God's attention. In the book *Humility: True Greatness*, C. J. Mahaney makes the following statement: "God is decisively drawn to humility. The person who is humble is the one who draws God's attention, and in this sense, drawing His attention also means attracting His grace—His unmerited kindness."[2]

Don't miss the significance here. Those verses in Isaiah 66

have the potential to be absolutely life-changing, for in them we're told how we can experience the unmerited grace of God. We're given the key to unlocking the treasure chests of God's grace. That key is humility. If we desire to experience the grace of God on a regular basis, we must cultivate humility.

What is humility? Again quoting C. J. Mahaney: "Humility is honestly assessing ourselves in light of God's holiness and our sinfulness."[3] God is holy. He's perfect in every aspect, and he dwells in brilliant, unapproachable light. He's glorious beyond measure, infinitely above us, and the only one worthy of our worship and adoration. We, on the other hand, are thoroughly sinful. We are weak little creatures with limited abilities who are absolutely dependent on God for every breath we suck into our lungs. In contrast with God, there is nothing praiseworthy in us. One glimpse of God in all his glory and majesty would utterly destroy us. The humble man understands that God is great and that he is not.

What is pride? Pride is when human beings try to be God. We are proud when we fail to acknowledge our dependence on God. We are proud when we desire the glory that belongs to him alone. Pride makes us glory thieves. When we're proud, we're seeking to steal the glory that belongs to God. God hates pride, and in James 4:6 we are told, "But he gives more grace. Therefore it says, 'God opposes the proud, but gives grace to the humble.'" He actively and passionately opposes the proud.

The application of these truths is simple. Do you want to experience the grace of God while playing sports? Do you want to attract the attention of God? According to Isaiah 66, one of the primary ways to do that is by being humble. If we desire to experience grace while on the playing field, we must first put on the jersey of humility.

What does a humble athlete look like? How do we know if we're being humble while playing sports?

First, the humble athlete recognizes God as the source of all athletic ability. A humble athlete realizes that his talent is an undeserved gift. Granted, most successful athletes put in hundreds of practice hours in an effort to sharpen their skills. The greatest athletes work until their muscles tremble and their heart booms like a cannon. They lift weights, run wind sprints, and beat their bodies into submission. But they are only sharpening the skills that God bestowed upon them. If God hadn't given them the ability to coordinate their arms, legs, hands, eyes, and mind, all their practice would be a colossal waste of time. Their efforts on the practice field would be pointless exercises. The humble athlete realizes that any athletic ability he has is a gift from God to be used according to his purposes.

What does this look like practically? At some point during or after each game that you play, pause for a moment and thank God for the wonderful gift of athleticism that he's given to you. You could have been born with a physical deformity that prevented you from playing sports. Instead God has given you a healthy body. Therefore, be very intentional about transferring all glory to God. If someone praises you for a job well done, thank him, but don't stop there. After he is gone, direct your heart to the Lord, and give him glory and honor. Let praise flow out of your mouth before the Gatorade flows into your mouth.

Second, the humble athlete encourages others. In Ephesians 4:29 we read, "Let no corrupting talk come out of your mouths, but only such as is good for building up, as fits the occasion, that it may give grace to those who hear." A proud person doesn't encourage other people because he's consistently self-focused. C. J. Mahaney comments on this by saying, "Where there's an absence of edifying words there's also normally the presence of pride and of self-righteousness, because those who are proud are too preoccupied with themselves and think too highly of themselves to care about building others up or to be sensitive to their true needs."[4] How often I find myself being a proud athlete! I think far too highly of myself. I'm quick to criticize my teammates and slow to encourage them. I'm very critical of their mistakes and very forgiving of my own. I say things in my head like, *If only they would pass me the ball more, we wouldn't be down by so many points!* How arrogant this is. The truly humble athlete encourages his teammates.

When you play sports with others, be intentional about encouraging them. If they're Christians, make it your primary goal to point out evidences of God at work in them. Encourage them for their outstanding attitude when the referee made a terrible call. Commend them for the way they humbly received correction from the coach. Highlight evidences of God's grace in their lives. After you've done that, encourage them for their performance as well. Rather than trumpeting your own successes on the playing field, draw attention to the ways your teammates excelled. Doing this will enable you to grow in humility and to experience the grace of God on the playing field.

Third, the humble athlete is team-oriented rather than me-oriented. He's more concerned with the success of the team than with personal achievement, even if it means playing less. A proud athlete, on the other hand, is passionate for personal glory and honor at the expense of the team. He loves personal stats and can instantly tell you his batting average, RBI total, slugging numbers, fielding percentage on Wednesdays, stolen bases during the month of August, and a thousand other stats. To put it another way, a proud athlete loves his own glory and is willing to sacrifice the good of the team for personal success. His primary concern is receiving the accolades that come with individual achievement.

What does it look like to put the team first? It looks like passing the basketball to a wide-open teammate instead of forcing a difficult shot. It looks like hurling your body into a defender to prevent him from sacking the quarterback. To put the team first means doing whatever it takes to ensure the success of the team, even if it means sacrificing personal gain. Philippians 2:3–4 instructs us in the following way: "Do nothing from rivalry or conceit, but in humility count others more significant than yourselves. Let each of you look not only to his own interests, but also to the interests of others." We are called to count other people as more significant and more important than us. Do you count others as more significant than you when it comes to playing sports? Who is your primary concern, yourself or your teammates? If we are to honor God when we play sports, it is essential that we be team players.

Finally, the humble athlete refuses to argue with the referees. In Proverbs 12:15 we are told, "The way of a fool is right in his own eyes, but a wise man listens to advice." A proud person is convinced that he's always right. He's absolutely certain that his perspective alone is correct and that anyone who disagrees is not only wrong but a complete idiot. A proud athlete is quick to disagree with questionable calls made by the referee. He feels quite sure that he's the final authority on what really took place on the playing field and doesn't hesitate to voice (usually very loudly) his opinion to the official. This disagreement isn't always loud, however. I've often found myself quietly, and pridefully, disagreeing with a call made by a referee. I may not be shouting or talking back to the ref, but my quiet disagreement is just as sinful. In my pride I believe that I alone saw the play correctly and that anyone who disagrees is a fool of historic proportions. In reality, I'm the fool. If I were humble I would realize that my perspective is limited and that I could easily be wrong. To believe that I'm always right is not only arrogant, it's absurd. I would also understand that referees make mistakes, just like I do. God has forgiven me of far more than a simple officiating mistake. I can honor God by overlooking the relatively insignificant mistakes made by referees.

THE PRIORITY OF PASSION

Imagine yourself as a sideline reporter in a Super Bowl. As you stalk the sidelines before the game, you happen to notice one team's starting quarterback doing stretches. You walk over to him, microphone extended like a sword, hoping to get a pre-game prediction. When you ask him how he feels about the game, he says something that completely shocks you. He says, "You know, I don't really care who wins this game. I mean, I guess it would be nice to win, but frankly I don't really care."

If a Super Bowl quarterback ever said this, you would probably begin to wonder how his team made it there in the first place. Championship teams are made up of the bloodiest, dirtiest, sweatiest athletes who give everything they have on the playing field. Athletes who play without intensity usually ride the bench while other, more intense players take their place. But as Christians we have to ask, is it right to play sports with passion? Does God care whether I play hard or not? Does it matter to God if my uniform gets dirty? We must turn to Scripture for the answer.

Colossians 3:23–24 tells us, "Whatever you do, work heartily, as for the Lord and not for men, knowing that from the Lord you will receive the inheritance as your reward. You are serving the Lord Christ." From this passage we learn that God is honored by those who work hard. We are commanded to work hard in whatever we do, whether that be studying biology, programming computers, digging ditches, or playing sports, as if we were working for God himself. Not only is it right to play sports passionately, but it brings honor to God! Compare this to the attitude of some athletes who say, "I only play hard when I want to" or "If I'm not getting the ball, I won't play hard." Such an attitude doesn't please God. God is glorified when we play sports with all the energy and intensity that we can muster.

I find the example of legendary Australian miler John Landy to be particularly provoking. In 1952 Landy was attempting to become the first man to run a mile in under four minutes, and his training regimen was absolutely brutal. Neal Bascomb describes Landy's efforts in his book *The Perfect Mile*:

> His agricultural science studies demanded that he train at night, after he had finished with his papers and reading. At eleven o'clock or past midnight he slipped quietly out of his house, making sure not to wake his parents or four siblings, who had little idea of the extreme effort he was making. Many nights it was difficult to force himself to put on his shoes and get out there. As he put it, "The mind is always selling out the body." He often rationalized that he was too tired and might better put off the run until the next day, or that he deserved a day off. But then he would convince himself to run at least a few laps. "It's like a car starting. There's an immense amount of energy you need to start a car, but once you're rolling, it's easy." Since he had returned from the Olympics, Landy hadn't missed a single training session: this was a pure exercise of the will.[5]

Later in the book we read the following about Landy's training techniques:

> An hour and a half into the [training] session Landy had usually run eight to twelve 600-yard laps at a pace of roughly ninety seconds each (or a sixty-five second 440-yard lap). Between each, he jogged a lap of the oval path in four minutes. He repeated these sessions—pushing himself to the limit of his physical abilities—five nights a week. On the remaining two

nights in the week he ran seven miles, sometimes more, at a five-and-a-half to six-minute pace, along the roads leading out of Melbourne. This was to build endurance. Regardless of weather, sore tendons, blistered feet, or fatigued muscles, Landy trained like this religiously.[6]

How contrary this is to many modern athletes! Very few athletes today have the courage to train with the same intensity as John Landy. To my knowledge, Landy wasn't running for the glory of God. He was running for himself and for Australia. If Landy was willing to batter his body for the glory of Australia, how much more should we who are Christians play hard for the glory of God.

Unfortunately, sinful motives often drive our passion. The desire for recognition or a sinful craving to win often turns our energetic play into nothing more than energetic self-worship. I often find myself playing hard because I want others to see me as an exceptional athlete (which I'm not). I want others to look up to me and whisper things like "He's probably the best athlete I've ever seen" as I pass by. I regret to say that my passion for my own glory usually drives me to play sports with intensity.

So what should be our motive for playing sports passionately? How do we do this without succumbing to pride? According to Colossians 3:23–24 we should work hard as if we were working for God himself. We should play sports as if Jesus Christ himself were standing on the sideline, coaching us. Sports aren't about us but about Jesus. Our intensity on the football field or tennis court should be fueled by a passion to please and honor Jesus Christ.

Oh, how this should affect the way we play sports! Knowing that we're playing for Christ himself shouldn't temper our enthusiasm but instead focus it. Before you step onto the court, remember who you're playing for. It's not for yourself, and it's not for your coach. You play for Jesus Christ, the glorious Savior and Redeemer. During the game, stop for a moment and ask yourself, would I be playing with more intensity or enthusiasm if Jesus Christ were the coach of my team? Would I be more encouraging to my teammates if I had to go back to the bench and sit next to Jesus? Would I argue with the referee if I had to turn around and look Jesus in the eye? Would I be angry with my teammates if I had to see Jesus face to face in the locker room after the game? I believe that stopping to consider these things can have a tremendous impact on the way we play sports.

So let us play sports with all the passion that we can summon, not for our own glory and honor, but for the honor of Jesus. Let us remember for whom we're truly playing, and let's play in a way that will bring him pleasure.

THE PRIORITY OF SELF-CONTROL

I remember it all very clearly. I was playing pickup basketball with a number of friends, and I was being covered by someone we'll call John (names have been changed to protect the innocent). John wasn't a basketball player. He was gangly, uncoordinated, and shot like a boxer that had taken one too many head shots. He was only playing because his friends were playing. But what John lacked in ability, he made up in effort. He covered me tight—too tight in fact—and he ended up hacking me repeatedly throughout the game. Now, normally I'm a pretty self-controlled person. I'm not known for angry outbursts or throwing punches at opposing players. But on that day something inside me snapped. As the game progressed and I continued to get fouled, I could feel the anger rising inside me like a swelling tide. Then the tide broke. I had the ball in my hands, and John fouled me for what seemed like the millionth time. Without a second thought, I took the ball and flung it at him with all my might, hitting him squarely in the nose. One minute we were all enjoying a friendly game of basketball, the next minute it felt like a murder scene. No, John didn't die. He was okay except for a tender nose. But in my anger I had murdered him in my heart. Playing basketball turned me into a spiritual murderer. Thankfully, by God's grace I was convicted of my sin and was able to ask John's forgiveness for my outburst.

Sports have a unique way of bringing anger out of us and causing us to lose all self-control. We've seen it on television. Bobby Knight flinging chairs across the court in a furious rage. Pittsburgh Steelers coach Bill Cowher, spittle flying and jaw jutting, screaming at his players as they step off the field. My favorite angry coach moment belongs to ex-Pittsburgh Pirates coach Lloyd McClendon. After being ejected from a game for arguing with an umpire, McClendon did what any reasonable coach would do. He walked over to first base, ripped it out of the ground, and stalked off with it into the team dugout. I'm not sure what he thought stealing first base would prove, but it did have an inspirational effect on his players. The Pirates rallied to win the game in extra innings.[7]

Scripture tells us that God's grace is "training us to renounce ungodliness and worldly passions, and to live self-controlled, upright, and godly lives in the present age, waiting for our blessed hope, the appearing of the glory of our great God and Savior Jesus Christ" (Titus 2:12–13). Many athletes have mastered their bodies but have not mastered their anger. They're seriously loaded in the talent department and seriously lacking in the self-control department. This shouldn't be the case for the Christian. If we're to bring glory to God when we play sports, we must learn to play with self-control.

Why do we become so angry when we play sports? In James 4:1–2 we find the answer. That passage reads, "What causes quarrels and what causes fights among you? Is it not this, that your passions are at war within you? You desire and do not have, so you murder. You covet and cannot obtain, so you fight and quarrel." Within each of us a fierce battle is raging. Our passions are at war. We crave and we don't get. We desire and we don't have. We become angry when we want something and we don't get it. Nobody can *make* us angry. John wasn't the cause of my anger. The source of my anger was within. Anger is the result of unsatisfied cravings. We want something and we don't get it, so we become angry.

What does this look like on the playing field? Let me paint a possible scenario for you. It's a beautiful Saturday afternoon and you, along with several friends, have decided to play a friendly round of golf. You confidently tee up your ball on the first hole, eager to demonstrate your golfing prowess to your golfing buddies. In one smooth motion you draw the club behind you, hold it for a brief second at the top of its arc, and then unleash a mighty swing that would make even Tiger Woods envious. You're filled with deep satisfaction as you watch the ball rise into the air and rocket forward . . . straight into the woods. With a mystified look on your face you turn to your friends and say, "Must have been a crosswind." They all nod knowingly. It's not a big deal because, after all, this is only the first hole. You'll prove yourself over the next seventeen.

On hole two things seem to be going a little better. You open the hole with a beautiful shot down the middle of the fairway and are set up with an easy chip onto the green. But your easy chip goes a little further than you intended, rolls down a hill, and settles nicely into a creek. You examine the head of your club closely and then throw it back into the bag, muttering, "Cheap clubs."

Holes three and four don't go any better. On hole three you take your eye off the ball, which causes you to hit a squib shot that only goes fifteen feet. Your golfing buddies let out a few restrained chuckles. On hole four you hit a duck. Literally. By some freak shot you manage to hit a duck sitting by one of the water hazards. The duck is fine, but you're not. You can feel the anger beginning to boil inside you. Your buddies are snickering a little more loudly by this point.

Hole five is a short par three, with no hazards, bunkers, or ducks. Surely you should be able to play this hole without any problems. You carefully tee up your ball and spend extra time visualizing your shot. In your mind's eye you can see the ball leaving the tee, traveling in a straight line down the fairway, and then landing gently on the green. With this image engraved firmly in your mind, you hit the ball.

Things don't go quite as you had imagined. The ball shoots off your club at a bizarre angle, nearly hitting one of your buddies, and lands thirty yards in front of you and 150 yards to your right. You've had enough. With a scream of rage you pound your club into the ground with all your might, intent on snapping the head off. You then give your golf bag a swift karate kick, scattering clubs, balls, and tees across the ground. When your rage is spent you stalk off in the general direction of your golf ball, muttering under your breath. Your friends aren't laughing anymore.

What was it that caused you to explode on the golf course? According to James 4, you wanted something and you didn't get it. In this case, you craved mistake-free golf and the approval of your golfing buddies. When your golf balls went flying into the woods and your friends laughed at your expense, you became angry.

Cravings are at the root of anger. What cravings cause you to become angry on the playing field? Do you become angry because you don't get enough playing time? Do you lose it when your teammates make mistakes? Do you become furious when a referee makes a poor call? In every case there's a sinful craving at work in your heart. You crave more playing time, causing you to become angry when you ride the bench. You want perfect play from your teammates and become furious at their mistakes. You want all the crucial calls to go your way and explode when a referee makes a bad call. You become angry when your cravings aren't satisfied.

So how should we respond when we find ourselves becoming angry? First, we must put off anger by identifying the sinful craving that's at work within our hearts. When we find that we're becoming angry, we should ask ourselves, *What is it that I'm craving right now? What do I want that I'm not getting?* Do we desire better play from our teammates? Do we desire more playing time? Do we want people to see us as outstanding athletes? Whenever we feel anger rising in our hearts, we should ask God to help us identify the sinful cravings that are at work within us.

Second, we must put the sinful craving to death and put on self-control. By the power of God's Spirit, we must kill our sinful cravings and master our anger. How do we do this? By crying out to God for help the moment we feel anger beginning to strangle our heart. In 1 Corinthians 10:13 Paul tells us, "No temptation has overtaken you that is not common to man. God is faithful, and he will not let you be tempted beyond your ability, but with the temptation he will also provide the way of escape, that you may be able to endure it." We can't overcome anger by our own strength. But God promises that in the midst of temptation he will be faithful to provide a means of escape. When the temptation to get angry seizes us, we must cry out to God for strength and deliverance.

When battling anger I also find it particularly helpful to remember gospel truths. I seek to remind myself of what I truly deserve. I don't have a right to a certain amount of playing time. I don't deserve to play with mistake-free teammates. I don't deserve to have all questionable calls go in my favor. Whenever I become angry, it's because I feel that one of my supposed "rights," such as the right to playing time, has been violated. In reality, I deserve the wrath of God. The minute I committed my first sin, I forfeited all rights to any blessing from God. He owes me wrath, not blessing. But in his incredible mercy, he doesn't give me what I deserve. Instead of crushing me, he crushed Jesus on the cross, and now he pours out undeserved blessing on me. Therefore, I have no right to be angry when things don't go my way or to lash out at teammates or referees when they don't meet my expectations. Instead I am called to put off anger and put on self-control.

Scripture tells us, "But the fruit of the Spirit is love, joy, peace, patience, kindness, goodness, faithfulness, gentleness, self-control" (Galatians 5:22–23). Attending anger management classes won't solve my problems. I need God's Holy Spirit to give me supernatural power. Without it I can't be truly self-controlled in a way that pleases God.

So how should we respond when things don't go our way and we feel fury building within us? We should begin by immediately confessing our sinful cravings to the Lord and repenting of them. This should be followed by crying out to God for the power to be godly athletes. God is eager to help us grow in the area of self-control. He's eager to pour out his Spirit on us so that we might live self-controlled lives for his glory alone.

THE PRIORITY OF TRUST

In the 2006 World Cup, Italy and France clashed to determine who would be crowned soccer champion of the world. With both teams playing stifling defense, the game ended in a 1-1 tie, and after two additional overtime periods the game was still deadlocked. It would come down to penalty kicks. Italy scored easily on their first penalty kick. France answered back with a goal of their own. Italy scored again, putting them ahead 2-1 in penalty kicks with David Trezeguet set to take the next kick for France. Trezeguet focused on the ball and prepared to take his crucial penalty kick. You could almost sense the entire nation of France willing him to drive the ball past the goalie and into the net. Trezeguet made his move, and the Italian goalie dove to one side of the net, hands outstretched, in a desperate effort to block the ball. Only he dove to the wrong side. Trezeguet had faked out the Italian goalie and had a wide-open net in front of him. With one swift motion he sent the ball screaming toward the net, backed by the screams of millions of French fans.

But their screams of excitement soon turned to screams of disbelief. Incredibly, the ball bounced off the crossbar and directly into the ground, just feet in front of the goal. Trezeguet had missed. He had a wide-open shot, and he missed. If only he hadn't kicked it quite so hard. If only he had tried for the bottom right corner of the net. If only he hadn't been so nervous. If only, if only, if only. Italy easily made their next two penalty kicks, securing their championship victory and their place in the annals of soccer history. Trezeguet and the entire nation of France could only watch in anguish as their hopes of soccer glory were dashed by a relatively thin piece of metal called the crossbar.

How does one recover from a letdown of such massive proportions? How does one recover after missing potentially the most important kick of a soccer career? These are questions that David Trezeguet would have to wrestle with in the upcoming months. Would he be tormented by his fateful missed kick?

Fortunately, most of us will never find ourselves in the same place as David Trezeguet. Most of us won't be called upon to make a game-winning kick in the World Cup or to avoid making the final out in the World Series. However, like Trezeguet, many of us will encounter disappointment in one form or another as we play sports, and our response to that disappointment will be determined by what we believe about God.

In Scripture we are informed that God is sovereign and rules over all things. He causes all things to work together for his good purposes; nothing happens outside of his sovereign plan. Even seemingly random events such as the casting of a lot (which today would be the equivalent of flipping a coin or tossing dice) fall under the sovereign control of God. Proverbs 16:33 tells us, "The lot is cast into the lap, but its every decision is from the LORD." Nothing falls outside of the sovereign rule of God.

If God is sovereign over the casting of the lot, then he's certainly sovereign over all that happens while playing sports. Every pitch that's thrown and every free throw is controlled by God's sovereignty. This should give us great comfort in times of disappointment or frustration. Everything that happens while playing sports is part of God's good and sovereign plan. If I hit the game-winning single and am carried off the field by my teammates, I should thank God for allowing that to happen. If I play a terrible game and let the game-winning hit trickle through my legs, I should still thank God for allowing that to happen. Why? Because we're told in Scripture that God sovereignly works all things together for the good of his people. Romans 8:28 says, "And we know that for those who love God all things work together for good, for those who are called according to his purpose." If you're a Christian, you can be absolutely confident that God is working everything in your life together for your good and his glory.

This truth should profoundly affect the way we play sports. If my team loses, I can trust that God allowed that to happen for my good and for his glory. If I play poorly, I can still rejoice because I know that God is working in that situation for my good and his glory. If I end up sitting the bench for an entire game, I can know that it was for my good and God's glory. God is sovereignly at work in all our circumstances, and for this reason we can fully trust him.

So where do you currently find yourself? Are you tempted to

gripe because you have sat the bench for the entire season? Are you sick with disappointment over your recent slump? Are you on a team that can't seem to win a game? All these circumstances have been brought about by God for your good and his glory. So instead of complaining about riding the bench, give thanks to God! The next time your team loses, take a moment to thank God for his sovereign work in your life. In doing so you'll bring honor to God and will experience the joy of trusting him.

THE PRIORITY OF DEPENDENCE

Independence is cool. At least that's what our culture says. We love to hear stories of athletes overcoming impossible odds by reaching deep inside and finding their "inner strength." Ultramarathoner Dean Karnazes, who has run 350 miles without stopping,[8] speaks passionately of this inner strength. In his book *Ultramarathon Man* he says:

> There's really no mystery to what I do, however. It hurts me just as bad as anyone else. I've just learned an essential insight: your legs can only carry you so far. Running great distances is mostly done with your head . . . and, as Benner [a previous running coach] taught me twenty-five years ago, your heart. The human body is capable of amazing physical deeds. If we could just free ourselves from our perceived limitations and tap into our internal fire, the possibilities are endless.[9]

Dean Karnazes echoes the attitude of our culture, which says that nothing is impossible for those who dig deep and find their "internal fire." Gatorade captures the essence of this attitude when they ask, "Is it in you?" Our culture loves self-sufficient, never-say-die, gladiator athletes who overcome all obstacles by sheer willpower.

But the Christian athlete should have a different attitude. Listen to the words spoken by David after he defeated all his enemies: "For you equipped me with strength for the battle; you made those who rise against me sink under me" (2 Samuel 22:40). David didn't defeat his enemies by tapping into his internal fire, nor did he overcome them with sheer willpower. David knew that his strength came from the Lord. We hear the same theme echoed in Isaiah 40:29–31 when the prophet says, "He gives power to the faint, and to him who has no might he increases strength. Even youths shall faint and be weary, and young men shall fall exhausted; but they who wait for the LORD shall renew their strength; they shall mount up with wings like eagles; they shall run and not be weary; they shall walk and not faint."

From these passages we learn that God is honored when we depend on him for both spiritual and physical strength. When playing sports we desperately need both. We need spiritual strength to overcome our pride, anger, self-sufficiency, and laziness. We need strength to exercise self-control when things don't go our way. We need strength to put to death our sinful cravings. Without supernatural spiritual strength from God, we'll never play sports in a way that pleases him.

We also need physical strength from the Lord. We need it when our lungs are on fire and our legs are quivering like gelatin. We need it when it feels like we can't practice another minute. We need it when every muscle in our body aches and we desperately want to quit. The truth is, we are not independent. We are weak, frail creatures who quickly fall apart. We desperately need God to provide us with both spiritual and physical strength.

Before the game begins, plead with God for spiritual and physical strength. Ask him to help you kill your sin. Ask him to give you the power of self-control and the grace to be humble. Confess your physical weakness to him as well. Acknowledge your absolute dependence on him for physical strength. Ask him to strengthen you for the "battle" you're about to enter.

Throughout the course of the game continue to appeal to God for strength. When you feel your heart bursting with sinful pride, cry out to God for his sanctifying power. When you feel your legs begin to shake from exhaustion, cry out to God for his strengthening power. Finally, when the game is over, thank God for the strength that he gave you. Taking these steps before, during, and after each game will help you grow in your dependence on God and to play sports in a way that brings him pleasure and glory.

AN ETERNAL PERSPECTIVE

The priorities that we set on game day will have an effect that lasts far beyond one game or even one season. They have eternal significance. One day each of us will stand before Christ to give an account of our lives. This truth should propel us toward holiness. In 1 John 3:2–3 we read, "Beloved, we are God's children now, and what we will be has not yet appeared; but we know that when he appears we shall be like him, because we shall see him as he is. And everyone who thus hopes in him purifies himself as he is pure." A day is soon coming when we will see Jesus Christ face to face. On that day I don't want to have any regrets. I want to know that by the grace of God I passionately pursued holiness. I want to hear him say, "Well done, good and faithful servant" (Matthew 25:21a).

Sports provide us with an opportunity to purify ourselves. When we grow in humility, passion, self-control, trust, and dependence, we become more like Jesus Christ. Therefore, let us resolve to pursue these things with all our might, knowing that one day we will stand face-to-face with our Savior.

CHAPTER FIVE

WINNERS AND LOSERS

Everyone has an opinion on winning and losing. For some people, winning is all that matters. "Winning isn't every-thing—it's the only thing," they say. For others, winning isn't quite so important. "It doesn't matter if you win or lose—it's how you play the game." Countless coaches have poured out their hearts in cramped, smelly locker rooms, hoping to rally their teams to victory and giving rise to famous phrases such as, "Win one for the Gipper." A sign hanging just outside the Notre Dame locker room reads, "Play like a champion today." On game day players slap the sign for luck just before running onto the field. Countless movies tell the story of hopeless underdogs rallying together to beat better, more experienced teams.

Something deep within the heart of man loves victory. We find ourselves gripped by movies that depict good triumphing over evil. In March 2006 the entire nation was riveted when little-known George Mason University beat basketball juggernaut University of Connecticut to advance to the Final Four in the NCAA Tournament. Victory is sweet, and defeat is terribly bitter.

Unfortunately, for every winner there's also a loser. For almost every person (except those who root for teams like the New York Yankees) defeat is a regular part of life. Those who are winners one year are often losers the next (or the next fifteen if you're the Pittsburgh Pirates). The ecstatic joy of winning is often quickly tempered by a string of losses. Losing is simply a part of life.

As Christians it's absolutely essential that we know what God says about winning and losing. If we're to live lives that honor God and bring him pleasure, we must learn how to biblically respond to both winning and losing. God has ordained that our lives be spent in both the winner's circle and the loser's bracket, and he wants us to learn how to please him in both places.

TO THE VICTOR GO THE SPOILS

Why is it that we experience such delight in victory? Why is it that something as simple as a game of one-on-one basketball between friends can quickly become an intense, all-out battle, with each man playing as if his life hangs in the balance? Why is it that I experienced such exquisite pleasure when my hometown football team (the Pittsburgh Steelers) won the Super Bowl in 2006?

We love victory. It thrills us and stirs our hearts. But is it right that we feel so? Is it right that we pursue victory? In Chapter 3 we concluded that victory is a reflection of God's character. God is a victorious God. Nothing can stand in his way; his plans can't be stopped. He always triumphs over his enemies, and we know that in the end, good will indeed triumph over evil. To desire victory is not necessarily evil. It's good and right that we strive for victory. We can catch faint, yet still delightful glimpses of the glory of God in the glory of victory, and this is what makes victory good.

Unfortunately, sin is still with us and taints even our most godly moments. Like a vile parasite, it clings to us in both victory and defeat. Specific temptations accompany both winning and losing, and we must be aware of how our sinful hearts work in both circumstances. We must learn how to enjoy the sweet pleasures of victory and how to endure the bitterness of defeat in ways that please God. Throughout the remainder of this chapter we'll seek to identify some of the temptations that accompany winning and losing and to determine how we might effectively fight against these temptations. Let's look first at the temptations that accompany victory.

THE TEMPTATION OF ACHIEVEMENT

One of the strongest temptations that accompanies any victory is to believe that we achieved it by our own abilities. If you listen carefully to a post-game interview with a star athlete, you will most likely hear the words *I* or *we* repeated over and over. "Yeah, we really came together as a team" or "I just played my heart out today. I left it all on the playing field." Our natural tendency and temptation is to take credit for any victory we achieve. This is a temptation that has plagued humanity for thousands of years. In Deuteronomy 8:11–18 we read:

> *Take care lest you forget the LORD your God by not keeping his commandments and his rules and his statutes, which I command you today, lest, when you have eaten and are full and have built good houses and live in them, and when your herds and flocks multiply and your silver and gold is multiplied and all that you have is multiplied, then your heart be lifted up, and you forget the LORD your God, who brought you out of the land of Egypt, out of the house of slavery, who led you through the great and terrifying wilderness, with its fiery serpents and scorpions and thirsty ground where there was no water, who brought you water out of the flinty rock, who fed you in the wilderness with manna that your fathers did not know,* that he might humble you and test you, to do you good in the end. Beware lest you say in your heart, 'My power and the might of my hand have gotten me this wealth.' You shall remember the LORD your God, for it is he who gives you power to get wealth, *that he may confirm his covenant that he swore to your fathers, as it is this day.* (emphasis added)

The Israelites faced the same temptation that we face today.

The Lord had brought them out of slavery, was leading them into a lush and wealthy land, and promised to prosper them if they would obey his commands. But the Lord knew that the Israelites, like us, are prone to pride and arrogance. He knew that they would be tempted to take credit for something that he alone had accomplished. It was the Lord who engineered their prison break out of Egypt and slaughtered the entire Egyptian army in the Red Sea. It was the Lord who led them through the terrifying wilderness and provided them with plentiful food and water. It was the Lord who brought them into the Promised Land, and it would be the Lord who would build their flocks and increase their wealth. The Israelites were clearly dependent on God to meet their every need. Unfortunately, even their spectacular escape from the hand of Egypt could not prevent Israel from being sinfully proud. In spite of all that God had accomplished on their behalf, the Israelites would still be tempted to believe they had achieved their great wealth by their own might and power. Therefore God warned Israel not to forget the source of their great blessings. He entreated them to remember the One who gave them power and might. He called them to remember their Deliverer.

We are no different than the Israelites. We too forget who gives us our strength and abilities. Like the Israelites, we're quick to take glory for something that was ultimately accomplished by God alone. Sports are prime examples of this. Look no further than your own life for the evidence. Where do your thoughts naturally go following a victory? If you're like me, you often find yourself thinking something along the lines of "Wow, I really played well today. I have some serious talent." Or perhaps, "Man, I was on fire today! I just couldn't miss. I think the other team was afraid of me. I was unstoppable." Just like the Israelites, we boast of what we think *we* have achieved.

THE TEMPTATION OF IMAGE

Another temptation that often accompanies victory is the desire to maintain a certain image. We want people to see us as winners, to think highly of us. We hope that they think thoughts about us like, "Wow, I want that guy on my team because he never loses." Winners get glory, and we desire that glory. Victorious athletes receive praise; losing athletes get criticized. Championship teams receive victory parades; losers get booed. If you're a good enough athlete you might even receive a nickname like "The Answer" or "The Beast." Bad athletes get nicknames too, but theirs don't sound nearly as intimidating. They get stuck with nicknames like "Spoon Hands" or "Greasy Fingers." Our hearts crave the honor that comes with victory. We want to be admired and well-respected. In short, we want to be praised. Our hearts desire glory, adoration, and honor, things that belong to God alone. Just winning isn't enough. We want an audience to witness our victories and then sing our praises after the game. We desire to be worshiped.

THE TEMPTATION OF VINDICATION

This was pointed out to me by a fellow pickup basketball player and good friend named Phil. He explained to me that many times after a victory he feels vindicated. "It feels like the high view I had of my talents and abilities was proven true by my victory," he said to me. How true this is in my own life as well. Most of the time I see myself as a pretty good athlete with above average talent. I have a decent jump shot and dribble fairly well. I'm relatively quick and can even pass behind my back if I need to. All in all, I'm the kind of guy you want on your team. Or so I think. For both Phil and me, winning seems to confirm that we truly are as good as we thought. We feel as though the victory came because of our out-standing play. Our perspective becomes distorted. We overlook the contributions of our teammates and turn a blind eye to our own blunders. Wallowing in our pride, we seriously overestimate our abilities. In essence, we become the object of our own worship.

What about you? How do you feel after your team has a convincing victory? Do you feel vindicated? Does victory cause you to stick out your chest with pride? Perhaps you, like Phil and me, struggle with the temptation of vindication.

THE TEMPTATION OF SUPERIORITY

For some, including myself, this may be the strongest temptation of all. By its very nature, sports lead to the exaltation of some and the humiliation of others. It thrives on mismatches. Talented teams consistently put a beating on weaker teams. The absurdly rich New York Yankees can afford to buy talent, while welfare teams like the Pittsburgh Pirates must develop talent within the organization. Sports are built upon the principle of inequality.

These inequalities can present a strong temptation toward sinful pride. After cruising to a convincing victory over a weaker team, we can be strongly tempted to believe that we're superior to those on the losing team. We'll acknowledge that they're talented, yes, but compared to us they're nothing more than posers. When discussing players on the other team, we may find ourselves saying things like, "They're not bad, but they're not that good either." In one form or another we end up looking down on them. When taken to the extreme, this may even lead a more talented athlete to mock a less talented athlete. Prior to a game between the Cincinnati Bengals and the Cleveland Browns, Bengals wide receiver Chad Johnson sent bottles of Pepto-Bismol to each of the Browns four starting defensive backs. Why? Johnson predicted that he would "make them sick" with his receiving.[1]

The temptation toward pride becomes even stronger in one-on-one sports. Beating other athletes single-handedly can make us prone to a "you can't touch me" attitude. Our prideful minds begin to run wild with crazy thoughts like, "Plain and simple, I'm the best. Ain't nobody can handle this player." We thump our chests and sniff our noses at the "amateurs" we just destroyed.

THE REMEDY

How do we combat the temptations discussed above? First, we must notice the common thread of sinful pride that runs through each of these temptations. Pride causes us to believe that our athletic success comes from our own powers and abilities. Pride causes us to strive to maintain a certain image in the hope of receiving praise from others. It gives us a distorted perception of our own abilities and causes us to feel superior toward those around us. In each case there's a sinful desire for glory and honor, a desire to be praised and worshiped, either by other people or by our own arrogant thoughts. This foul pride that's lodged within our hearts puts us at odds with God, for "God opposes the proud, but gives grace to the humble" (James 4:6b). The solution, therefore, is clear. If we are to enjoy victory in a way that pleases God, we must learn to win with humility. God is opposed to the proud and drawn to the humble.

So how does one cultivate humility in the midst of victory? How can we apply the healing salve of humility to our wicked and prideful hearts? To start, we must identify the sinful craving for worship that drives our desires for achievement, image, vindication, and superiority. Then we must crucify those desires through the application of humility. Let's examine how humility manifests itself in each of the four temptations mentioned above.

First, the humble athlete battles the temptation of achievement by recognizing that all success and achievement come from the hand of God. It's not by our own gutsiness or strength that we win championships or Most Valuable Player awards. Victory comes from the Lord. Proverbs 21:31 informs us that "The horse is made ready for the day of battle, but the victory belongs to the LORD." This isn't to say that practice is unimportant. In fact, practice is essential. The Christian athlete practices hard, doing drills over and over until he can perform the moves in his sleep. He runs sprints until the sweat pours off his body in great rivers. He punishes his body until he collapses in exhaustion. But ultimately all of our victories come from the Lord. He sovereignly determines the outcome of each game. He gives strength to our muscles and the hand-eye coordination necessary to move them. He sustains our heart as it pumps blood throughout our body while we sprint down the track. If the Lord desired, he could take away our athletic ability in a heartbeat. A little bleeding in the brain would instantly trash our athletic career. Therefore we have absolutely nothing to boast about. Any athletic feats that we've accomplished are from the hand of the Lord. Make time during your post-game celebration to acknowledge that it was God who gave you the victory. Don't make the mistake of assuming that you can win whenever you want. Rather, express your dependence on the Lord for victory before and after every game. In doing so you will honor the Lord.

Second, the humble athlete battles the temptation of image by realizing that only God is truly glorious. Compared to the infinite God, we are wretched little creatures indeed! Scripture tells us that God is the most glorious, radiant, incredible being that exists. First Timothy 6:15–16 describes Jesus Christ as "the blessed and only Sovereign, the King of kings and Lord of lords, who alone has immortality, who dwells in unapproachable light, whom no one has ever seen or can see. To him be honor and eternal dominion. Amen." Wow! Compared to Jesus Christ we are small, puny, wicked creatures. We don't have anything to boast about. Any glory we thought we had is nothing more than garbage when compared to the glory of Jesus Christ. In reality, we have no image to maintain because we're not glorious. Only Christ is glorious. Before and after each game, address your heart on this matter. Throw aside any desires for personal glory, and ask the Lord to help you long for his glory alone. Acknowledge that God alone is glorious and that you are nothing. Ask the Lord for a true vision of both his glory and your sinfulness. This will lead to humility on your part and to God being glorified in your victory.

Third, the humble athlete fights the temptation of vindication by realizing that he's little and weak. A true glimpse of God's glory will shatter any rosy thoughts we have about ourselves. After seeing the risen Christ in his full splendor, John said, "When I saw him, I fell at his feet as though dead" (Revelation 1:17). When Isaiah saw the Lord in the temple, he cried out, "Woe is me! For I am lost; for I am a man of unclean lips, and I dwell in the midst of a people of unclean lips; for my eyes have seen the King, the LORD of hosts!" (Isaiah 6:5). He's the Almighty King—we're weak bags of flesh and bones. He's the Maker of all things—we struggle to make a simple putt. Victory doesn't confirm our superior athletic ability. Rather, success is an undeserved gift to wicked sinners from a lavishly generous God. Don't allow a win to come and go without taking time to orient your heart toward the Lord. Following a win, humble yourself before the Lord and declare that he is awesome and you are not. Pray that God would give you a clear glimpse of his glory, and ask him to crush the serpent of pride coiled within your heart.

Finally, the humble athlete combats the temptation of superiority by realizing that God is infinitely superior to him. If we're tempted to feel superior to anyone, we're making the wrong comparison. We tend to compare our minuscule abilities to the abilities of those around us. This is like two wimpy nerds comparing the size of their biceps. Neither one is a tough guy, but one of them will come away feeling like a bruiser because he's got bigger guns. We do the same thing when we compare ourselves to others. In reality we should be comparing our might and strength to God's might and strength. Only then will we truly understand the greatness of God. The fact of the matter is, God is impressive and we're not. We may throw a football better than our friends, but we are by no means great. Furthermore, Scripture tells us that God isn't impressed by human might and strength. In Isaiah 66:2 God says, "But this is the one to whom I will look: he who is humble and contrite in spirit and trembles at my word." If you can swat a baseball 450 feet, does that make you something worth talking about? Maybe in the world's eyes, but not in God's eyes. That 450-feet blast won't capture God's attention like a humble heart. So if you find yourself tempted to believe the lie that you're superior to those around you, consider the greatness of your Creator. This will provide you with fresh perspective on what's truly impressive.

THE AGONY OF DEFEAT

Unfortunately, not everyone can be a winner. For every game-winning home run there's a pitcher banging his head against the shower wall. For every player doing a victory dance another player is angrily flinging equipment around the locker room. Sports are filled with moments of joy and moments of heartbreak. This was captured for me very clearly in the 2006 NCAA Men's Basketball Tournament, more affectionately known as March Madness. In the final seconds of a game between West Virginia (WVU) and Texas, a game in which WVU was down by twelve at the half, West Virginia trailed by a mere three points. They had one chance to tie the game with a three-pointer and send it to overtime. With only seconds remaining, center Kevin Pittsnogle took the ball at the top of the three-point line and launched a high arcing shot toward the basket, pleading with it to go in. The ball swished through the net, and the crowd went absolutely nuts. Only a few ticks of the clock remained, and it appeared that the game would go into overtime. Then the unbelievable happened. Texas in-bounded the ball to guard Kenton Paulino. Paulino received the ball past the half-court line, took several steps toward the basket, and catapulted a desperation shot. The shot went in, the clock hit zero, and West Virginia's hopes of a national championship were crushed. One minute the game was going to overtime, and the next minute it was over. The West Virginia players went from the highest of highs to the lowest of lows in the span of a few brief seconds. It was a painful loss to say the least.

At some point in our lives all of us will be losers. In fact, God has ordained losing to be a regular part of our lives. It reveals our character and exposes areas of sin that would lie hidden if we were always winners. It's one way in which God squeezes the sponge of our hearts to reveal the sinful cravings dwelling within. If we're to play sports in a way that pleases God, we must be aware of the temptations that come with losing. We will look at three.

THE TEMPTATION TO CRITICIZE

In 2005 the Philadelphia Eagles lost to the New England Patriots in the Super Bowl. Following the loss, a number of interviews were conducted with Eagles star receiver Terrell Owens. In these interviews Owens criticized team quarterback Donovan McNabb for his performance in that game. Owens claimed that McNabb had gotten tired at the end of the game, leading to poor performance when it mattered the most. Rather than praise McNabb for his outstanding performance and leadership throughout the season, Owens chose to stab him in the back. These comments essentially ended any relationship, shaky as it may have been, between the Philadelphia quarterback and receiver. Owens now plays for the Dallas Cowboys.

One of the strongest temptations following any loss is to criticize those around you. I'm a prime example of this. Following a loss I want to blame my teammates. I have thoughts like "My team couldn't hit anything today! They couldn't even make their layups. I was practically carrying the team myself." Or if I'm not criticizing my teammates I'm criticizing the officials. "Those refs stunk it up! We must have had three bad calls go against us." Sometimes I'm even tempted to come down on my coaches. "These coaches have absolutely no idea how to set a lineup. A monkey could make a better lineup than these guys." There's a strong temptation following any loss to blame those around you. We overlook our own mistakes and exaggerate the mistakes of our teammates. We seek to make ourselves look better by blaming the loss on the mistakes of others. I find that no matter how poorly I might play, I can always blame a loss on someone else.

THE TEMPTATION TO AGONIZE

A second temptation that athletes often face is the temptation to agonize over a loss, especially those that are particularly heartbreaking. I think back to one especially heartrending defeat that I experienced when I was fifteen. I was pitching for my junior legion baseball team and had been pitching very well throughout most of the game. I had excellent control, was throwing with a lot of zip, had a good curveball, and was feeling confident as the final inning rolled around. Then things started going terribly wrong. My pinpoint accuracy deserted me, and the plate seemed to have shrunk to the size of a postage stamp. Soon the other team had men on base and was threatening to score. I desperately tried to regain my earlier form, but it was all to no avail. The opposing team kept scoring, and I kept pitching like a drunken sailor. When all was said and done, I had singlehandedly cost my team the game.

The temptation after such a loss is to let your mind replay the game endlessly, wondering how you might have done things differently. Thoughts like "If only I hadn't thrown the ball over the first baseman's head" start to circle like vultures in your head. Despondency and self-pity can set in. All in all, such a loss can cause you to feel downcast and cheerless.

THE TEMPTATION OF SHAME

This temptation is closely linked to the previous one. Many athletes, including myself, may experience a sense of despondent shame following a loss. This can be an especially strong temptation for me if I've performed poorly during the game. I feel like I let my team down and imagine that they also feel I let them down. I envision my teammates discussing my performance, then shaking their heads in disgust and wishing I wasn't on the team. These thoughts usually lead me to make some sort of rash vow, promising myself that I will never perform poorly again. I know that I can't keep my vow, but it helps me feel better nonetheless.

REMEDY NUMBER TWO

Scripture isn't silent in addressing the temptations mentioned above. Once we identify the sinful desires that drive us to criticize, agonize, and suffer shame, we can put them to death with the truth of Scripture. Like a surgeon using a scalpel to remove a cancerous tumor, we must use the scalpel of Scripture to remove these sinful desires. Several truths will help us conquer these temptations.

First, we must realize that criticism is a fruit of pride. The proud man is quick to criticize those around him because he believes they make many more mistakes than he does. He foolishly believes that he's incapable of making the mistakes of his teammates. To put it another way, the proud man exalts himself above those around him. Criticism often flows out of a desire to exalt ourselves above others.

Jesus tells us, "Whoever exalts himself will be humbled, and whoever humbles himself will be exalted" (Matthew 23:12). When I criticize those around me, I'm seeking to raise myself above them by putting them down. This is wicked pride, and God passionately opposes it. He opposes it to such a degree that he promises to cut down those who seek to exalt themselves. If we're to please God when we lose, we must fight against the temptation to sinfully and arrogantly criticize our teammates.

A second truth that will greatly help us in the midst of a loss is the sovereignty of God over all things. In Romans 8:28 we read, "And we know that for those who love God all things work together for good, for those who are called according to his purpose." Agonizing over or being crushed by a loss is an indicator that we're not trusting God, who sovereignly arranges all things to work for our good. Every pitch and putt on the golf course, every ball thrown over nine innings, every free throw—all of them are woven together by the God who is working all things together for our good. The next time you find yourself disappointed by a loss, ask yourself, do I believe that God allowed me to lose for my good? If you find yourself agonizing over the details of a defeat, it's likely that you aren't trusting the sovereign God who cares for you.

The final truth that will help us in the midst of a loss is to realize that we have no image to maintain. Shame in sports is often the result of failing to meet the expectations of others. My teammates expect me to play well, and I don't want to let them down. I want them to think highly of me and praise my athletic ability. I desire their worship. When I don't play well, I experience shame.

I feel like I have the word *loser* branded onto my forehead. I don't receive the worship that I crave, and as a result I feel humiliated.

Scripture tells us, however, that God alone is worthy of worship. Losing allows us to see that we aren't as impressive as we thought. Our abilities are limited and our talents insignificant. In Romans 12:3 we read, "For by the grace given to me I say to everyone among you not to think of himself more highly than he ought to think, but to think with sober judgment, each according to the measure of faith that God has assigned." If we experience shame after a loss, it's probably because we thought too highly of ourselves. We shouldn't be surprised when we perform poorly. In fact, it's quite a foolish thing to think that we should always play excellently. If we truly saw how fragile we are and how great God is we wouldn't feel shame following a loss. We would realize that we simply aren't the incredible athletes we think we are and that only God is truly great.

THE BIG PICTURE

No matter how significant they may seem, all our wins and losses are very insignificant in the grand scheme of things. There are no lives hanging in the balance, nor is the peace of the free world dependent on whether we win or lose. God's kingdom will continue to advance even if our softball team doesn't. In terms of the big picture our wins and losses are pretty insignificant. We would do well to maintain this perspective.

Yet the battle against sin continues to rage within our hearts. In his kindness God allows us to experience both winning and losing, so that we might learn to conquer the sin that arises in both situations. In this way we will learn to play sports in a way that truly pleases the Lord.

CHAPTER SIX

PARENTS, CHILDREN, AND THE GLORY OF GOD

Twenty-five dollars. That's a lot of money to an eight-year-old boy. Enough to persuade him to act as a hit man against a younger teammate afflicted with autism, at the request of his coach. In the summer of 2005 a T-ball coach in Pennsylvania allegedly offered eight-year-old Keith Reese twenty-five bucks to intentionally hit autistic teammate Harry Bowers with the ball while warming up. Apparently the coach wanted to bench Harry because he wasn't good enough, but the coach was prevented from doing so by league rules, which state that each player must play for at least three innings. So the coach got dirty. First Reese hit Bowers in the groin with the ball. When that didn't have the desired effect, the coach instructed Reese to "go out there and hit him harder." Harry took a ball straight to the head.

Fortunately Harry wasn't seriously hurt, and the coach was brought to trial for ordering the assault. At the time of this writing the case is yet to be resolved.[1]

Stories like this are becoming quite common today. In 2001 Danny Almonte pitched a perfect game in the Little League World Series. Throughout the entire tournament Danny rung up an incredible forty-six strikeouts and gave up only three hits. He was a national sensation, and people were astonished at his performance—until they discovered that he wasn't twelve years old as he claimed—he was fourteen. His records have since been erased from the books.[2]

At a high school basketball game in 2004 a woman was ejected from the gymnasium by a referee for screaming obscenities at a player. Her husband, who happened to be a rather large fellow at six feet tall and three hundred pounds, disagreed with the referee and proceeded to body slam him to the ground. The husband faces up to two years in prison. All because of a basketball game.[3]

Playing sports is a learning experience for children. They learn how to swing a bat and shoot a basketball and tackle another person. But it goes much deeper. When children play sports, they learn values and priorities that will stay with them throughout their entire lives. In the heat of competition attitudes are forged. But these attitudes aren't formed independently. They are shaped by friends, parents, and coaches. Children are like sponges, soaking up everything that goes on around them. Values and priorities held by parents will be transferred to their children.

Proverbs 22:6 instructs parents to "Train up a child in the way he should go; even when he is old he will not depart from it." Sports are all about training. To be successful, an athlete must train diligently. The best athletes punish their bodies with torturous training exercises, seeking to harden their muscles and increase their endurance. Like sports, godliness doesn't come without training. Scripture calls parents to diligently train their children in the ways of the Lord, and sports provide a unique context for that training to take place. Our children won't learn to play sports in a God-glorifying manner apart from rigorous spiritual training. Just as my toothpick legs guarantee that I'll never dunk a basketball apart from intense training, our children's sinful hearts guarantee that they won't play sports for the glory of God unless they're trained in the ways of God. A child could spend hours learning to hit a baseball without achieving the slightest growth in godliness. As C. J. Mahaney says, "I fear that all too often our sons [or daughters] devote significant time to playing sports with little growth in godliness."[4] Throughout this chapter we will seek to identify specific ways parents can help their children grow in godliness while on the playing field. By the grace of God, there's much hope that our children won't simply play sports. Instead they'll play sports to the glory of God.

HELP YOUR CHILDREN SAVOR CHRIST

We were created to worship God. We were made to delight in and savor his glory. He's worthy of our utmost affections and deepest passions. The greatest command in Scripture is this: "You shall love the Lord your God with all your heart and with all your soul and with all your mind" (Matthew 22:37). But to our shame, we're quick to worship other things. Like an unfaithful lover, we give our passions to money, relaxation, work, recreation, houses, cars, sex, and a host of other things. Like an evil machine, our wicked hearts are constantly creating new idols for us to worship. Unfortunately, children are no different than adults. Their hearts are miniature idol machines, filled with a boiling, festering mass of sinful cravings and desires. These idolatrous desires rage within them, leading them to believe they won't be happy until these desires are satisfied. Something small and seemingly insignificant, such as the desire to play sports, can quickly become idolatrous. If it isn't addressed quickly, this desire can become all-consuming, stealing away any love they have for the Lord.

A sickeningly vast array of sinful desires and cravings may lie at the root of this idol. One cause may be a desire for worldly recognition. Good athletes get treated like superheroes, and a passion for this recognition may be swirling within your children's hearts. A longing to be around friends may be another. Maybe your children just want to have fun and think sports will satisfy this desire. Whatever the case, one common thread can be traced through all idolatrous desires: the belief that something other than God will bring ultimate satisfaction. The desires themselves aren't necessarily sinful. It's not wrong to want friendship or fun. It's wrong when we want them too much. How do we know if we (or our children) want something too much? If we're willing to sin to get what we want or if we sin when we don't get what we want. If I get angry when my desire is thwarted, the desire is idolatrous. My anger proves that I think something other than God himself will make me truly happy. Like a delirious castaway who thinks that drinking seawater will satisfy his thirst, my anger shows that I've been deceived into thinking I can find satisfaction in something other than Jesus Christ. It proves that something is terribly amiss within my heart.

Let me provide an example. When I was about thirteen, I became obsessed with hunting. Yes, I know it sounds odd, but I really wanted to hunt. I really, really wanted to hunt. All my friends hunted. I even knew some girls who hunted. But when I asked my parents if I could hunt with my friends, they said no. For some reason they didn't feel okay with immature thirteen-year-old boys carrying around deadly firearms in the woods without any adult supervision. Being a complete idiot at the time, I didn't see what the big deal was. I mean, it wasn't like we would be shooting at each other. At least not intentionally. I felt like I was being treated unjustly. I pleaded and argued with my parents. I got angry at my parents. I felt that if I couldn't hunt I couldn't be happy. As absurd as it sounds, that was how I felt. My sinful heart had seriously deceived me. I had created an idol out of hunting, and I was essentially bowing down before it. I was willing to be disrespectful and angry toward my parents if I didn't get what I wanted. At that point I needed a good dose of truth.

There will be many points in our children's lives when they'll feel exactly as I did. They will sinfully crave something. Perhaps they'll have an intense desire to play on the high school football team even though you don't want them to. Or maybe they'll long for the approval of their teammates to the point of compromising their faith. In moments like these, we need to help our children understand that true satisfaction is found in God alone. Nothing in this world will ever provide lasting satisfaction other than Jesus Christ. Not playing sports or winning a state football championship or hunting or anything else. Knowing Jesus Christ and following his ways is the only path to lasting joy. Without the gentle instruction of their parents, children won't understand this. Psalm 16:11 says, "You make known to me the path of life; in your presence there is fullness of joy; at your right hand are pleasures forevermore." A time will come when our children are thoroughly convinced that something other than the Lord will make them truly happy. At that time we must gently remind them of this truth. We must help them identify the sinful cravings that are at work in their hearts. We must help them see that the ways of the world never truly satisfy. Proverbs 22:15 tells us, "Folly is bound up in the heart of a child, but the rod of discipline drives it far from him." By the power of God, we must work to gently drive out the folly that dwells in our children. In doing so we'll honor God and help our children to do the same.

HELP YOUR CHILDREN SET GODLY PRIORITIES

The world sets the following priorities for athletes: success, victory, and personal glory. Every year athletes receive awards with titles like "Most Valuable Player" or "Defensive Player of the Year" that celebrate their athletic conquests. You'll never hear of a Major League baseball player receiving the "Most Humble Player" award or the "Most Unselfish Player" award. Why? The world is opposed to God and all of his ways. Rather than being honored and celebrated, godliness is often ridiculed. Humility is called weakness, and unselfishness is branded as a lack of ambition.

Children aren't exempt from the sinister influences of this world, and from an early age they'll be assaulted by its values. Just as a sea vessel requires a steady hand at the wheel to keep it from being blown off course, children require the steadying hand of godly parents to keep them from being influenced by the world's values. To combat the influence of the world, parents must help their children set godly priorities on game day. This doesn't mean simply attending our children's games and ensuring that they don't get into a screaming match with the umpire. It means intentionally preparing and instructing our children with biblical truth before and after each game. C. J. Mahaney, addressing fathers specifically, puts it this way: "It is our responsibility as fathers to teach and prepare our sons with biblical priorities prior to a game (or practice) and not to assume that we have fulfilled our fatherly responsibility simply by attending the game."[5]

What are these biblical priorities? Let's review the priorities we identified in Chapter 4, this time with a specific emphasis on our children.

Priority number one is humility. Scripture tells us that God is impressed by and attracted to humility. Our culture, on the other hand, only cares about performance and victory. You'll never see "The Top Ten Most Humble Plays of the Week" on ESPN *SportsCenter*. You'll definitely see the high-flying dunks and bone-splintering tackles, but you'll never see a highlight reel dedicated to humility.

Parents, we must help our children understand what's truly

impressive. God is impressed with the player who never gets into a single game and yet humbly hands out water to his teammates during timeouts. He's impressed with the player who takes time to encourage each of his teammates after a game. He takes notice of the athlete who, out of humility, clamps his mouth tight and doesn't argue with the referee over a questionable call. He isn't impressed with many of today's athletes who are both amazing and arrogant. We must help our children see the glories of humility as well as help them cultivate it personally.

What does this look like practically? First, help your children learn to transfer all glory to God for any success. Remind them that success comes from the Lord, and encourage them to give thanks to God for any success they might have. Second, encourage your children to diligently pursue correction from their coaches. Encourage them to intentionally seek out the coaches at the conclusion of each game and ask for input on how they might play better. Third, help your son or daughter select a sports hero. Our culture makes heroes out of athletes who aren't heroes in God's eyes. It idolizes loud-mouthing, flashy, self-glorifying athletes. Without instruction it's likely that your children will adopt one of these athletes as their hero. Help your child choose a hero who exemplifies humble, unselfish play. Finally, help your children assess their talent realistically. Our natural tendency is to sinfully and foolishly overestimate our talents, which in turn often leads to pride. With much gentleness and encouragement, help your sons and daughters realistically assess their talent. In doing so you'll help them avoid the pitfalls of pride that come when we overestimate our abilities.

This list is by no means exhaustive. My hope is that these practical suggestions will be a starting block for you as you seek to train your child in the ways of humility.

Following humility, the second godly priority is passion. In

Scripture we're called to do our work diligently, remembering that we're ultimately working for the Lord and not for men. God is well-pleased when we do our work wholeheartedly, with a passion for his glory and honor. But doing our work diligently isn't an easy task. Because of the sinful laziness within our hearts we're often tempted to give only a bare-bones effort, doing just enough to get the job done. We set minimal standards of excellence and feel content with mediocrity. This often carries over into sports as well. Practicing hard and playing hard require a tremendous amount of effort, and in our laziness we often end up doing both only halfheartedly. In doing so we fail to consider the interests of our teammates, who usually feel the effects of our sluggish play, and we fail to honor God, who is pleased when we work diligently for his glory.

We must help our children understand that practicing hard and playing hard are not ultimately about pleasing coaches but about pleasing Jesus. Christ is pleased when our faces gleam with sweat if our work was done with the aim of honoring him. He isn't pleased with the lazy or slothful athlete who does all he can to avoid hard work. These values must be impressed upon our children if they're to play sports for the glory of God.

The third godly priority that we must impress upon our children is that of trust. Remember how fragile a child's heart can be! Something small and insignificant, such as striking out to end a Little League game, can be devastating to young children. Their little world seems to come crashing down around them, and they feel as though they've let their entire team down. I've experienced failure of this sort many times and am familiar with the sense of shame that often accompanies it.

In these moments the truth of God's sovereignty can be an anchor for our children's hearts. Knowing that God loves them even more than Mom and Dad and cares about every little thing that happens to them can ease the pain of failure. On top of that, if our children have accepted Jesus as their Savior they can know that God makes everything that seems bad actually work for their good! Even when something terrible happens, like striking out to end a game, God is busily making it work for good. Parents, we must explain these wonderful truths to our children in terms they can understand. They may not understand what the word *sovereignty* means, but they can grasp what it means that God takes bad things and actually makes them work for good.

Learning these truths at a young age will greatly help our children as they grow older and experience trials far more painful than a strikeout. The truth of God's sovereignty will be an anchor for their souls in stormy times and a rich source of peace throughout their lives.

The fourth and final priority that we must impress upon our children is that of dependence upon God. How grateful I am that my parents taught me this truth at a young age. My final year in Little League was when I first truly learned the importance of depending on the Lord. The following words were written twelve years ago in one of my dad's journals:

> I will never forget how the Lord came through for Stephen. He didn't get a hit the first five games. And it seemed that the coach had some favorites he would play every game and in the infield, where Stephen really wanted to play. Stephen also wanted to pitch, but he wasn't even considered. Because he wasn't hitting, the coach would put him in only the minimum required time—one inning in the field and one at bat. Stephen would usually strike out. Oh those games were hard—for both of us. He'd come home feeling down—even cried a couple of times. I felt discouraged and really bad for Stephen. I'd really hoped his last year in the majors [the advanced league] would be good for him. So we began to pray and practice. We made

a rope-a-dope [a homemade hitting contraption] to practice hitting. We made a couple of trips to batting cages. I made a tee, which he hit at Getty Heights [a local park]. I also made a backstop in the backyard for hitting off the tee and doing "soft toss" hitting. Every game day I fasted for him. We prayed for favor in the coach's eyes. Finally, in the sixth game, I think it was, he got a line shot up the middle. The next game, his first time up, he struck out. The coach pulled him. Disappointed, I went for hot dogs, thinking he was out for the game. But then, in the fifth inning, the coach put him back in to bat. I couldn't believe it. Two strikes. Then Stephen hit one over the right fielder's head, knocking in the tying run. I think he scored the go-ahead run. Then in left field he caught the final out of the game. Afterwards, the coach said to me, "Mark, it was faith. I decided to follow my instincts, and something told me Stephen was going to get a hit. So I put him back in."

I'm quite confident that "something" was the Lord. I was a different ballplayer from that point on, both spiritually and physically. Sure, I hit better, and that was great. But more importantly, I learned to depend on God. Before each game my dad and I would pray together that God would help me play well. We prayed for a lightning bat and a sure glove, and we prayed that God would help me have a good attitude during the game. Those prayers had a lasting impact on my life. They taught me that I desperately needed God's help, even when I played sports. Praying taught me that all my abilities ultimately came from the Lord, and it taught me to give thanks anytime I played well. These truths continue to affect me to this day. Before I play any sport, whether pickup basketball or church league softball, I pray that God will enable me to play in a way that brings him pleasure. The truths communicated by my parents when I was young made a lasting impression on my life.

Parents, we must teach our children to be dependent on God

when they play sports. Most coaches teach their players to have a "buckle down and suck it up" mentality and a "believe in yourself" attitude. While these slogans make for nice T-shirts, they often lead to sinful pride and arrogance. Without biblical instruction our children will quickly adopt these sinful attitudes as their own. If our children are to play sports for the glory of God, they must learn to be dependent upon him.

HELP YOUR CHILDREN SEE THE BIG PICTURE

I was recently in Orlando, Florida on business and had the opportunity to go to Universal Studios with a friend. While there we decided to grab lunch at NBA City, a restaurant that doubles as a shrine of sorts to the National Basketball Association. As we approached the restaurant, my eyes couldn't help but be drawn to a statue of a basketball player that stood in front. The statue was massive, perhaps forty feet high, and it dominated the landscape. It was as if someone had constructed a golden idol to the god of basketball. I looked around for some expensive sneakers to sacrifice but couldn't find any. I suppose I'll be cursed with a poor jump shot for the rest of my life.

All silliness aside, the statue really does represent the current status of sports in our society. We worship sports. People sacrifice time, energy, and even their families on the altar of sports. We buy basketball shoes that cost as much as a small car and get cable packages that allow us to watch thirty-seven football games simultaneously. It's becoming somewhat difficult to determine which holiday is more significant to our country, Christmas or Super Bowl Sunday. Parents are spending millions of dollars and thousands of hours to help their children get the extra edge on the playing field.

All this begs the question, is it really that important? Don't get me wrong, I absolutely love sports and enjoy them as a gift from God. But in light of eternity, do they matter all that much? Does it really matter who wins the Super Bowl or the pennant race or the Daytona 500? It's very easy for both us and our children to get caught up in sports fanaticism, often to the neglect of other, far more significant areas of our lives. As Christians we must strive to maintain a biblical perspective on sports and to help our children do the same. Without this perspective our children may place too high a priority on sports while neglecting things that are far more important. What are some of these things? We'll examine just a few.

The first and highest priority in the life of our children should be their relationship with God. This takes precedence above all else. Sports, though not inherently wrong in any way, can have a poisonous influence on our children's walk with the Lord. Often playing on a sports team means spending large chunks of time around non-Christians, both on the field and in the locker room. Many teams practice for several hours every day, resulting in our children spending a significant amount of time with those who aren't following the Lord. In 1 Corinthians 15:33 we read, "Do not be deceived: 'Bad company ruins good morals.'" As parents we must use discernment before allowing our children to play sports. If we believe that our children's relationship with the Lord may be harmed by playing on a certain team, we must not let them play. It's not worth it! No sport is worth sacrificing our children's relationship with the Lord. If we do let them play, we need to find out what's going on in the locker room and on the playing field. We should ask our children what kind of discussion takes place on the bench and what kind of language they're hearing on the playing field. We must help them guard their hearts against the influence of this world.

A second priority in the life of our children should be family. The family was created by God for his glory, and raising a family in the fear of the Lord requires spending time together on a regular basis. This time together should be unhurried, where parents can be both friends and teachers to their children. Without this unhurried time it will be difficult for parents to effectively communicate biblical truth to their children.

If not kept in check, sports can rip a family apart. Dad has to take one son to soccer practice and then run across town to watch his daughter's softball game. Mom is taking the youngest to swimming lessons but is running late because she has to pick up the oldest from water polo camp. Time spent together as a family goes out the door as various members go to their separate sporting events. Many times children don't realize the importance of spending time together as a family. They don't understand that sports often drive a wedge into a family, splitting parents and children apart. It's critical for parents to communicate to their children the importance of family over sports.

A final priority in the life of our children should be the church. Unfortunately, more and more sporting events are being played on Sunday these days, and it would be very easy for parents and children to miss a month of Sundays simply because of playing in soccer tournaments or hockey games.

The church was created by God to play a key role in our growth as Christians. In Hebrews 10:24–25 we're told, "And let us consider how to stir up one another to love and good works, not neglecting to meet together, as is the habit of some, but encouraging one another, and all the more as you see the Day drawing near." If we're going to experience growth as Christians, it's absolutely essential that we be involved with a church. Not just nominally involved, but passionately committed to corporately worshiping and hearing the preaching of God's Word on a regular basis. Our children should understand this priority as well. They must understand that the church takes priority over sports. It should be clear to them that fellowship with the saints is more important than friendship with teammates and that the preaching of God's Word is more significant than a pep talk from their coach.

What message are we sending to our children? Do our children understand the importance of the local church, or have sports become their priority? Do we and our children miss church on a regular basis due to sports commitments? If so, I believe the Lord wants us to reexamine our priorities. We must strive to make the church a priority for our family. Without the church our spiritual growth will stagnate, and the spiritual life of our family will suffer. Within the church both we and our family will experience the grace of God in a unique way on a weekly basis. We must clearly choose the church over sports.

ALL BY GRACE

If you're at all like me, reading a chapter like this can present a strong temptation to feel condemnation. When you compare all that you're supposed to be doing to all that you're actually doing, it's likely that you'll find yourself seriously lacking.

At this point we must once again look to Jesus, who hung upon a cruel Roman cross and received God's wrath for our sins. We must remember that our acceptance by God is not based upon how effectively we train our children but upon the perfect obedience of Christ. God accepts us and delights in us because of what Jesus accomplished, not because of what we've accomplished. If our failures as parents are hanging over us like a black cloud, we should turn to the Lord and receive fresh forgiveness of sins and fresh grace to train our children in the ways of the Lord. He's eager to forgive us and eager to help us grow. Effective parenting begins at the foot of the cross.

CHAPTER SEVEN

TYING IT ALL TOGETHER

The tension was so thick you could almost taste it. Anticipation hung in the air like a thick cloud, and each person in the room pulsed with nervous energy. Several general managers had laptops open and were studying the screens intently, analyzing charts and graphs. One manager flitted about the room like a nervous mosquito, haggling with other managers about various trade possibilities, then returning to his seat to shuffle through various player lists. A few of the managers were doing last-minute research, flipping through loose sheets of paper and dog-eared books in an effort to determine the perfect draft pick. This was draft day after all, perhaps the most important day of the year after Christmas and the Super Bowl. A manager who drafted well might win a championship. A manager who drafted poorly would be verbally harpooned by the other managers. Draft day was big.

For a brief moment everyone in the room was quiet. Then the commissioner uttered those words that both terrify and thrill the heart of every manager: "You are now on the clock." The words hung in the air for what seemed like an eternity. All eyes were fixed on one man. For several seconds he said nothing, relishing his position. Then with an air of power and authority he said, "With the number one overall pick in the 2006 draft, I select Larry Johnson."

From that point on the draft was fast and furious. With the

second pick I selected Shaun Alexander, who was quickly followed by LaDainian Tomlinson. After each pick, other managers would chime in, either approving of or mocking the selection. Chargers tight end Antonio Gates was selected in the second round, which as every manager worth his salt knows was way too early. The manager who selected Gates was instantly bombarded with a series of scathing remarks that questioned both his ability to manage a team and his manhood. But the jokes were not mean-spirited. It was all part of the game. This was the official Lord of Life Church Fantasy Football Draft.

A casual observer would have noticed two things about the men gathered together that day. First, they took the fantasy football draft very seriously. The winner of the Lord of Life Church Fantasy Football League was entitled to some serious bragging rights, and selecting the right players in the draft was essential to putting together a championship team. The second thing a casual observer would have noticed was that each man was having the time of his life. There was a sense of passion and unbridled joy in the air. Everyone in the room absolutely loved football and was delighted to be able to express their passion through fantasy football. It was like Christmas in September.

GOAL #1: ENJOYING A GIFT

My aim in this book has been to communicate two truths about sports. First, sports are gifts from God for our enjoyment. The Lord of Life Fantasy Football League is pure pleasure for me. Draft day is exciting. I love trying to assemble the ultimate fantasy football machine, capable of destroying any and all opponents. I get excited about studying game day matchups and individual player statistics. It's not drudgery for me to participate in the fantasy football league.

Consider for a moment all the joy that we receive from playing, watching, discussing, and reading about sports. Every Thursday (with the exception of one week out of the year) I eagerly anticipate receiving and reading the newest issue of *Sports Illustrated*. Every weekend from September until December I look forward to watching my beloved Pittsburgh Steelers and then discussing the game's highlights with my coworkers the following morning. The NCAA Men's Basketball Tournament has turned March into an almost sacred month for me. The list could go on. *Monday Night Football*. Thanksgiving Day football. The World Cup. The World Series. All are sources of joy for me. They are gifts from a lavish God.

We don't deserve to receive such joy. We deserve the wrath of God. Our sins merit his eternal, furious, and unending wrath. But we don't get what we deserve. Instead of consuming us with his wrath, God poured it out upon Jesus. When Jesus hung upon the cross, bleeding, broken, and marred beyond recognition, he was receiving the wrath of God for the sins of all who would trust in him. Now when we hope in Jesus for salvation we don't receive wrath. Instead we receive unmerited mercy and grace. We're brought into a relationship with God, and he calls us his children. Instead of being our judge he is our Father, and as our Father he loves to pour out blessings upon us. The best of these blessing are spiritual. We receive forgiveness of sins, a clean conscience, and power to change. Best of all, we come into close fellowship with God himself.

Furthermore, our attitude toward the other gifts of God changes as well. Before our conversion we treasure the gifts much more than the Giver. We love sports, food, music, and sex far more than we love the God who created these things. At conversion our passions change. Our passions for the lesser pleasures of sports, food, music, and sex are overshadowed by an all-consuming passion for the one true and glorious God. He becomes our first love, and we can enjoy the gifts of God as he intended us to enjoy them: for his glory.

God has given us the gift of sports so that we might enjoy them for his glory. Our athletic abilities were given to us by God so that we might use them for his glory. Let's not receive these gifts passively! Millions of people enjoy the gift of sports without ever uttering a word of thanks or praise to the glorious Giver of gifts. As Christians we know the author of every good and perfect gift. Let us resolve that whenever we're enjoying sports, whether playing or watching them, we will thank our extravagantly lavish God who gives us such wonderful gifts. May Colossians 3:17 echo in our minds before we step onto the playing field: "And whatever you do, in word or deed, do everything in the name of the Lord Jesus, giving thanks to God the Father through him." The next time you find yourself caught up in the joy of sports, take time to give thanks to the Lord, who is so generous in his gifts.

GOAL #2: SEIZING AN OPPORTUNITY

The second truth is that sports are opportunities. Ninety-nine percent of us will never be professional athletes. Yes, I realize that many of the men reading this book feel they could have gone pro in their prime. I hate to break it to you, guys, but most of us (myself included) simply aren't that good. And the older we get, the worse we become. I'm only twenty-four years old, but I can already feel my athletic abilities declining. In previous years I could play sports for hours without feeling any muscle soreness the following day. Now just a few games of pickup basketball make me feel as though I was in a minor car accident.

Even though we will never be professional athletes, sports still provide us with tremendous opportunities—opportunities to gain something far more valuable than a scholarship to a major school or a multi-million-dollar shoe contract. Sports provide us with opportunities to grow in godliness. Few things allow us to grow in humility, conquer our anger, discipline our bodies, persevere in the face of adversity, and pursue excellence, all in the span of an hour or two. Sports expose our sinful pride and desire for personal glory. They reveal our sinful self-sufficiency, self-worship, and self-centeredness. They also present unique opportunities to grow in humility, a character trait that deeply pleases God. Sports also expose our anger, impatience, and sinful cravings, thus enabling us to grow in God-honoring self-control.

However, growth in godliness won't begin automatically the moment we step onto the field. The process of growing in godliness, also known as sanctification, requires intentional effort. Just as an athlete must work hard to improve his skills, so we must work hard to grow in godliness. And just as an athlete must cooperate with his coach to improve his skills, so we must cooperate with the Holy Spirit if we are to be sanctified. As Christians, we have God's Spirit at work within us, speaking to us, moving us, and convicting us of our sin. We in turn are called to respond to the Spirit's prompting, repenting when we are convicted of sin and aggressively putting to death the sinful desires that wage war within us. Sports provide us with a wonderful opportunity to respond to the conviction of the Holy Spirit.

Recently I was playing pickup basketball with a number of people, including my younger brother. During the game he and I got tangled in several physical battles for rebounds, with a lot of pushing and shoving under the basket. Even though the pushing and shoving was simply part of the game, I could feel anger rising in my heart as it was taking place. With every push he gave me, I wanted to push back harder. I wanted him to know that he couldn't just shove me around. He was a barbarian invader into my territory, and I wanted to prove my superiority.

Fortunately, by God's grace, I didn't lash out physically at my younger brother. Unfortunately, I didn't exercise self-control over my tongue. At one point during the game I made several derogatory, angry comments to him in front of everyone else. I chided him for being "overly aggressive" and told him to be more careful, thus humiliating him in front of the other players. I didn't make these comments out of a desire to help my brother play better basketball or out of concern for his safety. I made them out of pride and anger.

Shortly after I made these comments I began to experience conviction from the Holy Spirit. In his kindness, God made me aware of my pride and anger and led me to truly repent. He also led me to approach my brother after the game and ask his forgiveness for my sinful words. As usual, he quickly forgave me.

That day a basketball game became much more than a basketball game. A simple game turned into an opportunity for me to put my sin to death and grow in godliness. If my memory serves me correctly, I didn't play very well that day. My shot was terrible, I drove to the basket like I'd just gotten my learner's permit, and I didn't score many points. But it didn't really matter. Something much more significant had taken place. I became more like Jesus Christ.

My hope is that after reading this book you no longer view sports as simply putting a ball through a hoop or slapping a puck into a net but as wonderful, God-given opportunities to grow in sanctification. Let us resolve not to play sports passively but to take full advantage of the opportunities they provide. Before you step onto the playing field, ask God to help you play sports in a way that brings him glory. Ask him for conviction of sin and for the power to put that sin to death. Parents, you can help your children in this area as well. Don't simply drop them off and pick them up from practices and games. Don't think that your responsibility ends with attending games. Rather, before each practice or game take a few moments to help your children prepare their hearts. Remind them of the need for humility, self-control, passion, encouragement, and trust. Help them see how sports fit into the bigger picture of life, eternity, and God's glory. If time permits, pray with your children before each practice or game. In doing so you will help your children grow in godliness while playing sports. Hebrews 12:14 tells us to "Strive for peace with everyone, and for the holiness without which no one will see the Lord." Sports provide us with an opportunity to strive for holiness. Let us take full advantage of that opportunity.

A CONCLUDING PRAYER

Father, thank you for sending your precious Son to die in our place that we might have a relationship with you. We deserve to receive your wrath and judgment, and yet you pour out mercy and kindness upon us. Through the blood of Jesus you have made it possible for us to live lives that are pleasing to you and to bring you glory. Please teach us to live in such a way. Teach us to delight in you above all other things and to love you, the Giver, far more than we love any of your gifts.

Yet, Lord, we thank you for the wonderful gifts that you pour out upon us. There is no one as generous or lavish as you. Thank you for the absolutely delightful gift of sports. What joy we receive from playing and watching and discussing sports! You are kind to give us such joy. Teach us to enjoy the gift of sports in a way that brings you pleasure and honor. Let us see that every talent and ability we possess is from you and for your glory. Help us to see beyond the gift to you, the extravagant, lavish Giver.

Thank you, Lord, for the wonderful opportunity to grow in godli-

ness that sports provide. Please empower us to take advantage of this opportunity and to pursue holiness with all our might. Help us see that holiness matters much more than performance and that godly character is of much greater value than athletic ability.

Father, we confess our inability to enjoy sports in a way that brings you pleasure apart from the power and grace that you provide. But, Lord, we are confident that because of the cross you will provide us with everything we need to live lives that bring you pleasure. We pray all this in the precious name of Jesus. Amen.

APPENDIX

By C. J. Mahaney

FATHERS, SONS, AND SPORTS

Last year as March Madness approached and my family began our annual ritual of filling out brackets, my friend Ligon Duncan asked me how I lead my son, Chad, as he plays and watches sports.

My friend asked a crucial question, for we are raising our sons amidst a culture that idolizes sports. And while it's often been said that sports build character, any perusal of the sports page reveals that it is also an arena for arrogance, immorality, and all kinds of public (and publicly excused) sin.

The following thoughts are by no means a thorough biblical overview of sports. But I hope they provoke us as dads to intentionally train our sons (and daughters) to glorify God when it comes to sports.

Each March, each new sports season and indeed each game our sons play or we watch together is an occasion that calls for wise parenting. It is an opportunity to lead our sons—to help them cultivate godly character and not simply develop athletic skill.

As my son well knows, prior to my conversion, playing sports was all about me. It was a means of self-exaltation, a way to draw attention to myself and pursue glory for myself. But I want Chad to be different. I want him to glorify God (and not himself) when he plays sports. And I want him to apply discernment when he watches sports.

He's a teenager now, but from a young age I have sought to dissuade Chad from emulating my past sinful example and to build into his soul an appreciation for playing and watching sports as a gift from God.

FATHERS, SONS, AND WATCHING SPORTS

When Chad and I watch a game together, I am on the lookout for ways to teach him. I want to equip him to discern true greatness in the eyes of God. True greatness, according to the Savior, is serving others for the glory of God. It is defined for us in Mark 10:43–44: "Whoever would be great among you must be your servant, and whoever would be first among you must be slave of all."

Nowhere is the word *great* mentioned more often in our culture than in the context of professional sports. If you watch any game this weekend and listen to the announcer's commentary, then like a mantra you'll probably hear the word *great* repeated throughout—great, great, great. Yet it may well be that nowhere in our culture is the *absence* of true greatness more evident than in professional sports.

Now, I'm not opposed to professional sports. I'm a longtime fan of the Washington Redskins and the Washington Wizards. But I hope I'm a theologically informed and discerning fan. And I want to teach my son to be as well.

So I never watch a game passively. I'm never just observing. Not only do I always have the remote ready to change the channel when a commercial comes on, I seek to draw Chad's attention to any evidence of humility or unselfishness I observe, as well as any expression of arrogance or selfishness. I will celebrate the former and ridicule the latter. For, more than anything, I want my son to celebrate and pursue *true greatness* in the eyes of God.

FATHERS, SONS, AND PLAYING SPORTS

Playing sports holds great potential for growth in godliness for our sons, but only if we as fathers lead our sons theologically and strategically. I fear that all too often our sons devote significant time to playing sports but fail to grow in godliness as a result.

Here is where the example and leadership of a father can make all the difference. It is our responsibility as fathers to teach and prepare our sons with biblical priorities prior to a game (or practice) and not to assume that we have fulfilled our fatherly responsibility simply by attending the game.

And after the game we should encourage and celebrate evidences of godliness and not primarily our sons' athletic ability or achievements.

Our priorities for our sons' participation in sports must be theologically informed priorities rather than culturally celebrated priorities. Fathers who aren't theologically informed are more impressed with athletic ability, statistics, and final scores than they are with biblical masculinity and godly character.

So, prior to each practice and game (Chad plays soccer and basketball) I have a conversation with my son about how he can glorify God. Here is a sampling of the biblical priorities and practices I review with him:

- Humbly receive correction from your coach, and ask your coach how you can grow in character as well as athletic skill.
- Thank your coaches for the way they have served you. And thank the referees after each game.
- Encourage your teammates for their display of godly character and athletic skill—in that order of priority.
- Encourage your opponents during and after the game. If you knock someone over, extend your hand to help him up.

- Play the game passionately and unselfishly. Serve your team by playing aggressive defense [his father never did this] and passing the ball on offense [again, his father never did this].
- Humbly respond when the referee calls a foul on you. Do not complain or disagree in word or by facial expression [unfortunately, his father always did this].
- No inappropriate celebrating after you score; instead recognize that others played a role [his father never did this].
- Thank the team manager for the way he served, and recognize the humility and servanthood he is displaying at each game. Remember that true greatness is sitting on the end of the bench.

There is nothing original or profound about this list. But helping my son apply it to his heart and life can make a profound difference.

After each game, I review the above list with my son. I go over the game with him and celebrate any and all expressions of humility and godly character I've observed. I tell him that this is more important to me than how many points he scored or whether his team won the game (although we do play to win!).

Remember, fathers, whatever you honor and celebrate, your son will emulate. Therefore, we must celebrate godly character more than athletic ability or achievement.

My passion for my son as he plays sports is that he would please and glorify God. I want him to grow in godliness, not simply in athletic ability.

You see, Chad will never play professional sports. His participation in sports is temporary and meant to be preparatory. Like his father, he will inevitably grow old and will only be able to walk for recreation or play golf poorly.

But by the grace of God, sports can help him grow in godly character and prepare him for manhood. His participation in sports can equip him to fulfill his calling as a man to humbly and courageously serve and lead in the home, church, and culture.

For that to happen, though, I must teach my son to discern true greatness as he watches sports and to adopt biblical priorities and practices while he plays sports. Then, and only then, can we as father and son truly enjoy sports to the glory of God.

C. J. Mahaney

NOTES

CHAPTER 1: A LIFE FOR THE GLORY OF GOD

1. John Piper, *Don't Waste Your Life* (Wheaton, IL: Crossway Books, 2003), 31.

CHAPTER 2: THE SOURCE OF ALL TALENT

1. David Halberstam, *Playing for Keeps: Michael Jordan and the World He Made* (New York: Random House, 1999), 173.

CHAPTER 3: THE JOY OF SPORTS

1. *Chariots of Fire,* Warner Brothers Pictures, 1981; Warner Home Video, 1992.
2. C. S. Lewis, "Meditation in a Toolshed," in *C.S. Lewis: Essay Collection and Other Short Pieces* (London: HarperCollins, 2000), 607.
3. "The Catch (American Football)"; http://en.wikipedia.org/wiki/The_Catch_%28 American_football%29 (accessed January 4, 2008).
4. John Piper, *The Hidden Smile of God: The Fruit of Affliction in the Lives of John Bunyan, William Cowper, and David Brainerd* (Wheaton, IL: Crossway Books, 2001), 112.
5. Geoffrey C. Ward and Ken Burns, *Baseball: An Illustrated History* (New York: Alfred A. Knopf, 1994), 454–458.

CHAPTER 4: GAME DAY PRIORITIES

1. Mark Fainaru-Wada and Lance Williams, *Game of Shadows: Barry Bonds, BALCO, and the Steroids Scandal That Rocked Professional Sports* (New York: Penguin Group, 2006), xv–xvi.
2. C. J. Mahaney, *Humility: True Greatness* (Sisters, OR: Multnomah, 2005), 20.
3. Ibid., 22.
4. Ibid., 121.
5. Neil Bascomb, *The Perfect Mile* (New York: Mariner Books, 2005), 72.
6. Ibid., 73.
7. "Pirates Rally in 11th, Snatch Victory in 12th," *Pittsburgh Post-Gazette*, June 27, 2001; http://www.post-gazette.com/pirates/20010627buc0627p2.asp (accessed December 27, 2006).
8. See http://www.thenorthface.com/na/news/news-2005-10-12.html (accessed January 23, 2008).
9. Dean Karnazes, *Ultramarathon Man* (New York: Penguin Group, 2005), 231–232.

CHAPTER 5: WINNERS AND LOSERS

1. "Chad Sends Message in a Bottle," *The Cincinnati Post*.

CHAPTER 6: PARENTS, CHILDREN, AND THE GLORY OF GOD

1. "Boy Testifies Against Coach," *Pittsburgh Post-Gazette*, July 29, 2005; http://www.post-gazette.com/pg/05210/545643.stm (accessed December 27, 2006).
2. See http://en.wikipedia.org/wiki/Danny_Almonte (accessed December 27, 2006).
3. "Dad in Basketball Fight Faces Additional Charge," *Pittsburgh Post-Gazette*, March 18, 2004; http://www.post-gazette.com/pg/04078/287429.stm (accessed December 27, 2006).
4. Together For The Gospel Blog, "Fathers and Sons and March Madness"; http://blog.togetherforthegospel.org/2006/03/let_the_madness.html (accessed December 27, 2006).
5. Ibid.

SCRIPTURE INDEX

GENERAL INDEX

Stephen Altrogge is part of Sovereign Grace Ministries, a family of churches passionate about the gospel of Jesus Christ. In addition to this book, Stephen has written songs featured on several albums from Sovereign Grace Music. Find out more at www.SovereignGraceMusic.org.

In a Little While
The first father-son album from Sovereign Grace Music. Features songs written and sung by Stephen and his father, veteran songwriter and pastor Mark Altrogge.

Savior
More than a Christmas CD, *Savior* includes twelve songs focusing on the Incarnation. Each song is truth-saturated and singable, most of them suitable for use in corporate praise. www.SaviorCD.com

Valley of Vision
Worship songs inspired by the classic book of Puritan prayers, *The Valley of Vision*. Includes songs from Bob Kauflin, Mark Altrogge, Stephen Altrogge, and others. www.ValleyofVision.org

Worship God Live
Released in 2005, our first live CD in six years was recorded with worship leaders Bob Kauflin and Pat Sczebel. It includes 14 songs, each one rich in the glorious gospel and grace of our Lord Jesus Christ.

SOVEREIGN GRACE®
MUSIC

www.SovereignGraceMusic.org